Papers given at a Colloquium on Greek Drama in honour of R. P. Winnington-Ingram

On 16 March 1985, the Society for the Promotion of Hellenic Studies held a one-day Colloquium on Greek Drama in honour of Professor R. P. Winnington-Ingram, distinguished scholar and President of the Society 1959–1962.

In the course of revising their papers for publication, most speakers changed the titles of their contributions: 'Mothers' Day. A note on Euripides' *Bacchae*' by J. Gould was originally entitled 'The return of the *Bacchae*'; 'Notes on tragedy and epic' by P. E. Easterling was 'Tragedy and the heroic'. The paper by R. G. A. Buxton was given at the Colloquium as 'Doors and other boundaries in *Alcestis*'; this paper has also been published in *Dodoni*, to which Journal we offer our thanks for permission to reprint. 'Some problems of a translator' by S. A. Barlow began as 'Some problems in translating Euripides' and parts of this paper will appear in Dr Barlow's forthcoming translation of the *Trojan Women* for Aris and Phillips Ltd.

The sad death of T. C. W. Stinton some weeks after the Colloquium left us without an edited text of his paper. We are therefore particularly grateful to Mrs Sylvia Stinton, who supplied a revised version of 'The apotheosis of Heracles from the pyre' from among her late husband's papers.

LYN RODLEY

Contents

The apotheosis of Heracles from the pyre

The finest living interpreter of Greek tragedy, whom we are honour-
ing today, has given us, amongst many other good things, the best
book to date on Sophocles. In his illuminating treatment of the
Trachiniae, Professor Winnington-Ingram approaches with great caution the question whether the pyre of Heracles alludes to his
deification.[1] It has been left to another distinguished tragedian, Mrs
Easterling, to give the most subtle and sophisticated answer to this
question so far: that there is such an allusion, but that there is much
more to it than that.[2] I argue elsewhere in a forthcoming paper that
there is no such allusion to be understood from the play, though there
is indeed much more to it than that.[3] I am not here concerned
directly with the *Trachiniae*, so much as with the myth of Heracles'
apotheosis from the pyre, its significance and its development. But the
ultimate object of this enquiry, my ulterior motive as it were, is to try
and determine, as well as informed guesswork will allow, the attitude
Sophocles' audience might have had towards the legend, and what
response he might therefore expect from them.

In later antiquity the significance of the myth was not in doubt: the
pyre burnt away Heracles' mortal part and so allowed his immortal
part to ascend to godhead on Olympus. So Lucian's Hermotimus
compares the philosopher's abandonment of bodily goods, whereby
'shedding and divesting himself of all these he rises upwards', with 'the
way they say Heracles was burnt up on Oeta and became a god. For
he too, discarding everything human he has had from his mother,
with the divine element pure and untainted, separated out from the
fire, flew up to the gods.' Much the same idea underlies the account of
Heracles' death in Ovid, Seneca and Quintus Smyrnaeus,[4] and is
implied by Theocritus, Callimachus, possibly Plautus, Cicero, Livy,
Pliny and Minucius Felix.[5] The principle is fully expressed by
Iamblichus, and applied by Galen to Asclepius, Dionysus and others,
besides Heracles.[6] The 'meaning' of the myth, then, is that Heracles'
apotheosis was achieved by the burning away of his mortal part; as

Kirk puts it: 'it is a reasonable as well as a common conclusion that the mortal parts of Heracles nature were consumed by fire so that the immortal parts might be free to ascend to heaven'.[7] On a synchronic or structural interpretation, to which the evidence of every period is relevant, this is doubtless correct. But if our aim is to gauge the response of Sophocles' audience to the *Trachiniae*, we are concerned with a diachronic or genetic account, to show how the various versions developed.

Two such accounts have found favour. (I) Purification by fire leading to apotheosis was in fact the original meaning of the legend.[8] Apotheosis without the pyre, found in Hesiod[9] and on sixth-century vases,[10] will be either an incomplete or simplified variant, or an alternative 'Olympian' version, the logical sequel to the labours, both because they earned it, and because the last two (the apples of the Hesperides and the Cerberus labour, cf. the wounding of Hades and wrestling with Thanatos) symbolize the conquest of death.[11] The main stream—pyre leading to apotheosis—from which only *Trachiniae* deviates, is resumed in a series of vase-paintings beginning mid-fifth century (the two earliest, *c.* 460–450, are fragmentary, but their significance is clear from the whole scene depicted on the Munich pelikē, dating from the late fifth century.[12] It emerges in literature in a chorus of Euripides' *Heraclidae* (910 ff.), as usually interpreted: 'Your son, my lady, is gone up to heaven; his body burned in the flame, he escapes the report that he went down to the House of Hades'; and is triumphantly manifest in the *Philoctetes* (727–9); 'to the company of the gods came the bronze-shielded man, all bright with the fire of god.'[13]

This account is supported in two ways. Firstly (1) by analogy with other legends immortality is brought about either (*a*) by burning, e.g. the infant Demophon, whom Demeter tried to immortalize through putting him in the fire, and as Thetis tried with Achilles,[14] or (*b*) by lightning, e.g. Asclepius, Semele,[15] later conflated with the pyre in the Heracles legend. But (*a*) children are not the same as the moribund Heracles, and a constant feature of such attempts to immortalize is their failure: there is no analogy in Greek belief for immortalizing the dead or the adult living by burning.[16] Rejuvenation by boiling, etc., which is sometimes compared, is again different, since it does not involve breaking the barrier between mortal and divine.[17] At its simplest, old age, like disease, is seen as an accretion,[18] which can be boiled away, as in the rejuvenation of the sausage-seller in Aristophanes (*Eq.* 1321); though Medea's success with Aeson, Jason and (in a satyric context) the nurses of Dionysus and their husbands seem to have required magical adjuncts.[19] (*b*) As for lightning, its effect is to invest its target with an uncanny power: it makes *sacer* the person or place struck. In myth this may mean apotheosis.[20]

Secondly (2), the account is supported by analogy with oriental practice: (*a*) gods equated with Heracles (Melqart) at Tyre, Sandon at Tarsus); (*b*) the self-immolation of, e.g. Sardanapalus or Croesus; (*c*) Hittite kings, who became gods through cremation. (*a*) The equation with Melqart, the Tyrian Heracles, is made by Herodotus;[21] it is based on a rough analogy between the relevant beliefs and rituals, which do not include burning on a pyre. In fact, the ritual burning of Melqart is not well attested, the evidence being either late and possibly contaminated by the Greek legend, or ambiguous.[22] The evidence for a pyre-ritual of Sandon is weaker still.[23] (*b*) Sardanapalus is an example of suicide by burning,[24] but not, without unwarranted assumptions, of apotheosis, and is in any case too remote from Greece; Croesus lies nearer to hand, but *ex hypothesi* cannot have influenced the *origin* of the Heracles legend (see below). (*c*) The Hittite kings are a fair analogy,[25] but though Hittite influence on Greek myth or ritual is likely enough in the Mycenaean period, this analogy can hardly have been at work several centuries later.

The other account (II) of the pyre/apotheosis legend, and one now widely held, places its origin in cult. Farnell took it to be post-Hesiodic, and reluctantly accepted an oriental origin on the reasonable ground that no relevant ritual, such as the periodic burning of a god in effigy on Mt. Oeta, could be found as a starting-point for a purely Greek legend.[26] Just such a cult, it seemed, was being unearthed as Farnell wrote by Greek excavators, who discovered on Mt. Oeta a sacrifical site, possibly bronze age in origin, with bronze figurines, and sherds inscribed 'Heracles' dating from *c.* 600.[27] Nilsson assigned this to a type widespread in Greece and in Europe generally, often on the tops of mountains, shown by modern analogies and the Greek evidence to be used for ancient annual fertility rites, in which effigies were sometimes burnt.[28] Heracles, he concluded, had taken over an existing ritual as the god burnt in effigy, and the legend was an aetiology of his cult, probably originating in the seventh century.

The generalized explanation, derived from Mannhardt, that all such fire-rituals were fertility rites for the promotion of crops, is now inadequate; though Burkert's argument, that the ritual on Oeta cannot have been annual because the only relevant (and much later) evidence refers only to a *four-yearly* agon[29] will not do either: this evidence does not tend to show that the *pentetēris* was the *only* festival there. Nilsson's main contention, that Heracles took over a pre-existing ritual, has, however, been generally accepted. It is not clear that it favours a purely Greek origin for the myth; as Burkert observes, the combination of death by fire and deification recalls oriental practice, though how this became linked with the ritual on Mt. Oeta is a mystery.[30]

A third account (III), I would suggest, is equally plausible. Heracles is above all a hero. The nature of his deeds may set him apart, but they remain *heroic exploits* in the tradition.[31] It is as a hero rather than as a god that he might be expected to take over the fire-ritual on Oeta, one of a series whose cults came into being in the eighth and seventh centuries, probably through the influence of epic.[32] For a hero-cult taking over from such a pre-existing ritual Nilsson compares Coronis at Titane.[33] The aetiology, thus far, is that the fire-ritual on Oeta commemorates the funeral-rite of a great local hero; cremated, on the model of a Patroclus and in the manner of the times; appropriately in a sanctuary of Zeus, for he had no tomb; a repeated rite, the distinguishing mark of a hero-cult. Heracles died, in the earliest explicit account, from the poisoned robe,[34] and this is perhaps the most likely point for his connection with the fire-ritual on Oeta. I have assumed that the legend of Heracles' apotheosis, and his cult as a god, is not earlier than the seventh century, the *terminus post quem* being given by the Iliad, in which he unambiguously dies. If the apotheosis dates from the sixth century, a view which Professor West has recently reaffirmed,[35] then either the local cult on Oeta is the origin of the apotheosis in legend and in cult generally, which is highly improbable, or it follows that, as I am arguing, Heracles took over the cult on Oeta as a hero, and originally the pyre can have had nothing to do with his becoming a god.

The spectacular rite now feeds back into the myth the heroic act of *self*-immolation, which has several functions: (*a*) Heracles, like Ajax, seeks to avoid shame.—the shame of death at a woman's hands (a prominent theme in the *Trachiniae*; (*b*) heroes die violent deaths:[36] (*c*) Heracles, like Rasputin or Frankenstein's monster, is invulnerable to the extent that normal means cannot kill him;[37] (*d*) only fire will free him from the clinging robe and from the agony which in itself is shameful.[38] Suicide by burning is not a Greek practice, as Farnell observes, but it is sometimes found in myth: Evadne, Laodamia, Broteas the hunter; also—a real person, if not a historical example— Empedocles.[39] Finally, the kindling of the pyre by Philoctetes allows him to acquire Heracles' bow, as Odysseus acquired Eurytus' bow (*Od* 21. 31–2); this inheritance is not implied in Homer, nor in the Cycle.[40]

My account now becomes more speculative, though I hope not

unreasonably so. At some stage, perhaps from the first, the ritual on Oeta is augmented by four-yearly games (*Σ Il.* 22. 159); so the dead at Plataea were honoured by four-yearly games, as well as the annual fire-sacrifice (Plutarch, *Aristid.* 21), and Pelops by the Olympian games. But four-yearly games are for gods, not heroes; the games at Plataea are ostensibly for Zeus Eleutherios (Strabo, 412), and those at Olympia for Zeus also, though sometimes referred to as Pelops' alone (B. 8. 30 f.)[41] So here, perhaps, the games in honour of Heracles, though reasonably ascribed to him in *Σ Il.* l.c., were ostensibly for Zeus Oetaeus (referred to in *Trach.* 1191, possibly by his title Hypsistos, as in *Phil.* 1289).[42] The holocaustic sacrifice, if such it was, can hardly have been for Zeus as well (though a holocaust to Zeus is attested);[43] the analogy is again Coronis, whose fire-ritual took place in the temple of Athena (Paus. 2. 11. 7).[43a]

This somewhat speculative hypothesis is not, however, essential to my argument, for two reasons. Firstly, there are no good grounds for believing that the *penteteris* dated from the beginning of Heracles' association with the pyre, or even that it was introduced very early.[44] Any time after Heracles had been recognized as a god as well as a hero, both rituals in his honour, the annual and the four-yearly, could have taken place on Oeta.[45] Heracles was worshipped both as a god and as a hero in several places (Thebes, Sicyon, Cos, Thasos); in Thasos the two rituals took place in the same sanctuary.[46] This need not surprise us. Thre is no fundamental cleavage between Olympian and Chthonic cults; rather 'we are dealing with an antithesis within the ritual, not with two fundamentally different things,' which explains why a hero is sometimes worshipped in the same sanctuary as a god.[47] So too, it seems, when the same person is worshipped under both aspects.

Secondly, Heracles, like Asclepius or Amphiaraus,[48] is a special case: their cult as gods is wholly consistent with their death in legend. This need not surprise us either. The 'antithesis within the ritual' makes room for the coexistence of conflicting presentations of myth, and of apparently inconsistent attitudes towards them.[49]

Finally the death on the pyre (Acusilaus, 2 F 32) is reconciled with the story of the deification and ascent to Olympus. In Herodotus (7. 197) the spring Douras gushes forth to assuage Heracles' pain. In the earliest version in art (the fragmentary mid-fifth century depiction of Heracles on the pyre, see n. 12), the presence of Athena means that not only is his pain assuaged by the nymphs, named as springs in the Munich pelikē,[50] but that he is rescued and translated, as explicitly in the pelikē.

This may, I suggest, have been inspired by the story of Croesus, by now well known in the Greek world, witness a red-figured amphora depicting his pyre and its extinction, and the narrative of Bacchylides.[51] In Bacchylides' version,[52] Croesus puts himself on a pyre—and his family with him, like Sardanapalus—a pyre then extinguished by Zeus, whilst he, for his piety, that is, for services rendered to Delphi, is translated by Apollo while still living to the land of the Hyperboreans, a form of immortality. If the nymphs are clouds on the earlier vase-paintings of Heracles on a pyre, as they are on a fourth-century painting of Alcmena on a pyre,[53] the parallel is closer still; they will then be the agents of Zeus, whose function as sender of rain is naturally associated with mountain-tops.[54] In Euripides' *Alcmena*, which the painting doubtless represents, Zeus intervenes himself to avert the punishment of the innocent Alcmena by her outraged husband; the pyre and its extinction being perhaps modelled on the pyre of Heracles, perhaps, again, directly on that of Croesus.[55] Aeschylus probably had Heracles die on the pyre in the *Heraclidae*, arguably similar in plot to the *Trachiniae*.[56] whether or not the play mentioned apotheosis, and there is no indication either way, it could well have led to the vase-painters choosing the pyre as a subject.[57] The oriental model desiderated by Farnell is now given, how it entered into Greek myth is explained, and the mystery felt by Burkert still to be left by the discovery on Oeta is solved.

Clearly this account of how the legend developed is no more than a hypothesis, but it has some advantages. (1) It dispenses with Nilsson's assumption that Heracles' take-over of the fire-ritual involved his burning in effigy, for which the sole analogy, that of Hera at the Daidala, can only be represented as an annual rite by special pleading.[58] (2) It explains the oriental features of the myth without recourse to remote or implausible analogies. (3) It accounts for the existing evidence. If Nilsson's view (II) were correct, as is now widely held, we might expect so spectacular a reconciliation of Heracles' death with his divinity to have left some trace in art or literature before the mid-fifth century. That it did not could be due to decorative fashion or accident: there are known to be lost epics in which it might have figured, notably the *Capture of Oechalia*—though again it might not, as Burkert pointed out.[59] It might even have figured in Aeschylus. But, precarious as arguments from silence must always be for Greek myth and literary history, we are bound to rely on the evidence we have. It must again be stressed that quite apart from the genetic account, the *divinity* of Heracles in *cult* is, like that of Asclepius, wholly consistent with his *mortality* in *legend*. I would therefore hesitantly conclude that it is more likely than not that mention of the pyre would not have suggested apotheosis to Sophocles' audience.[60]

In the second part of my paper, I try to show that the notion that the process of deification was achieved through purification by fire of Heracles' mortal part was not likely to have been already current in the fifth century. The deification, like the translation of Croesus, is in the paintings a rescue from a pyre which must be extinguished: it is not effected *by* the pyre, as in Ovid, Seneca or Lucian. Nor is it so in E. *Hcld.* 912–14, on the most natural interpretation: 'he escapes the report that he went down to the House of Hades, his body consumed in the dread flame'—pyre, that is, still leads to death. S. *Phil.* 726–29 'to the company of the gods came the bronze-shielded man, all bright with the fire of god', has none of the 'like-to-like' implications it might have in Seneca (or even, in other connections, in Euripides): it means simply that Heracles was fresh from the fire of Oeta, and Oeta is sacred to Zeus (so Jebb).⁶¹ The ritual is at night, with the flames 'knocking at Heaven's gate', as Pindar says of the sacrifice for Heracles' sons at the Theban Heracleia.⁶² The earliest references to fire as a means to immortality, purifying the immortal part by destroying the mortal, are Hellenistic, first in Theocritus and Callimachus.⁶³ A similar development can be seen in Apollonius' account of Thetis' attempt to immortalize Achilles, where the means are explicit, as compared with the vagueness of the otherwise similar account of Demeter's attempt to immortalize Demophon in the Homeric hymn, which is either its model or its congener.⁶⁴ The elaborate joke seen by Housman in Plautus *Rudens* 766–68: 'I shall make a great fire here'—'So as to burn away your inhuman part?' (by burning out the inhuman part Labrax would at least humanize himself)⁶⁵ would, if he is right, presuppose a New Comedy audience familiar with the idea; for Plautus' audience the exploit of M'. Acilius Glabrio in 191 climbing to the top of Oeta 'where the mortal body of the god was burnt' (described by Livy) might even have made it topical.

The idea is in fact generally held to be old, at least as old as the pyre on Oeta and the Homeric Hymn to Demeter. This belief is apparently based on the projection into the archaic period of later evidence and modes of thought, and on the conflation of different kinds of myth. Thus Rohde can say that the destruction of the body to release the soul not only explains the 'meaning' of cremation (comparing the Rigveda), but also 'lies at the root of the stories of Demeter and Demophon, ... and also that of Thetis and Achilles, when the goddess, laying the mortal child in the fire, was stripping off his mortal flesh, and destroying his mortal part' (i.e. in the words of Apollodorus).⁶⁶ In the Homeric Hymn, Demeter tries to make Demophon 'ageless and immortal' by giving him ambrosia and putting him on the fire at night, is interrupted and so fails. There are various ways fire could assist the transition from one state to another, just as there are with cremation, which assists the transition from life to death. One such function is to annul pollution. Rohde quotes Archilochus fr. 9, 10–11: 'if Hephaestus had furnished his head and lovely limbs with a pure garment . . . ' (of a body lost at sea) to show that cremation purifies by consuming the mortal parts. But any funeral rite, burial no less than cremation, annuls the pollution of the unburied dead. Here the language itself shows that 'stripping off' and thus purifying the mortal part' is not the symbolic meaning intended (contrast Empedocles' image of 'souls clothed in an alien garment of flesh', B 126).[67] The meaning that is shared by the Demophon and Achilles myths is that human beings cannot acquire immortality.

The later mode of interpretation for the apotheosis from the pyre, as for the Achilles and Demophon myths, is established by the third century. Doubtless it started earlier, perhaps already late in the fifth: before that, however, there is no trace of such attitudes to death or immortality. I can only summarize briefly the complex factors which might have contributed to this development. First, some factors which might seem relevant but are not so. (1) The cathartic function of fire in cremation (see above). When Euripides speaks of the bodies of the Argive dead being 'purified in the fire' (*Suppl.* 1121), this does not imply 'stripping off the mortal part' any more than Archilochus fr. 9 did. Contrast a late sepulchral epigram in which the dead man 'having purified his body in a pure flame, departed to the immortals', which doubtless does imply it.[68] (2) The purification of Heracles by torches in the Eleusinian mysteries; Burkert compares the purification of the Proetids by Melampus 'with one torch and one squill' (Diphilus fr. 126 K).[69] Again, this has nothing to do with destroying the mortal part: the initiates did not acquire immortality.[70] (3) Oriental influence (other than the analogies with Heracles dealt with above). Zoroastrianism abhors cremation as a defilement. The Upanishads speak of the flame of the funeral pyre sending the soul up to heaven, but this is too remote: Brahminism does not impinge on the Greek world till the time of Alexander, whose guru Kalanos immolated himself.[71] It might be thought that the idea of the soul ascending to heaven in the flames is a natural one which could have established itself independently in the archaic and classical Greek world. But the evidence clearly shows that the Greeks regarded cremation and burial as equally effective means of transition from life to death, and did not believe that a preference for the one or the other would affect their chances in an after-life.[72] (4) The mystical apprehension of soul freed from body by shaman-type figures such as Abaris, Aristeas, Epimenides and Hermotimus, who practised levitation or absented themselves from their bodies. Er and his successors, who had visions of the after-life during a brief period of clinical death—usually twelve days—are akin to these.[73] (5) Pythagoras and Empedocles, grouped with the former by Dodds (l.c. [n. 73]), have more claim to relevance. The doctrine of metempsychosis, ascribed to Pythagoras himself, implies the immortality of soul, first mentioned explicitly by Herodotus in connection with this doctrine, which he says is Egyptian and had been adopted by a few individual Greeks up to his time. The implication was probably not fully worked out by then; as Burkert remarks, 'What appears in the fifth century is not a consistent doctrine of metempsychosis, but rather experimental speculations with contradictory principles of ritual and morality, and a groping for natural laws'.[74] Empedocles did in fact hold that the body was a cloak of flesh stripped away at death, in his own case by fire.

Marginally relevant is (6) the happy after-life anticipated by Eleusinian, Orphic or Dionysiac initiates. this is of a different order from immortality and must not be confused with it. But the persistence of a fully conscious soul again has implications which were probably not formulated in the fifth century, and are first fully worked out in the *Phaedo*. Possibly relevant is (7) death as the beginning of new life. Two lines of thought converge: (i) 'Who knows if this which we call life is death, and death is life?'[75] (ii) 'That which thou sowest is not quickened, except it die'; this principle may underlie Eleusinian ritual and beliefs, but how early it acquired an eschatological significance—death is the necessary condition for happiness hereafter—is quite uncertain.[76]

Nearer to hand is (8) heaven-bound soul distinguished from and opposed to earthbound body: 'aether received their souls, earth their bodies', on the dead at Potidaea, the oldest such epitaph extant; a notion especially favoured by Euripides, though perhaps already emerging in popular belief.[77] But the sepulchral epigrams, the best evidence for such beliefs, show that the idea was not widespread before the end of the fourth century; in fact only one other example can be dated with confidence before 350.[78] *Odyssey* 11. 218–22, to the effect that fire subdues flesh, bones and sinews, cited by Rohde as early evidence, certainly implies separation of the soul at death from a body which is destroyed by fire, but the point is that the dead in Hades have no strength or substance.[79] (9) Body as an impediment to the soul's progress towards betterment and immortality, summed up by σῶμα σῆμα.[80] Akin to this is the ideal of purity from bodily desires popularly associated with Orphism (as in E. *Hipp.* 953) and emphasized by Plato, notably in the *Phaedo*. (10) The roots of

Stoicism, including (8) (heaven-bound soul opposed to earthbound body) and (9) (body as an impediment to the soul's progress). 'The Stoic view of death appears to have been a variant upon the conception of soul as a stranger resident in the body, with additional stress on the fiery nature of its substance', as Lattimore put it.[81] The idea of a divine fire which survives the matter it consumes readily accommodates Heracles' apotheosis from the pyre, though individual immortality is a complication in Stoic doctrine. The Stoic contribution to the legend of the Phoenix, that it is reborn from its own ashes, which is clearly akin to the apotheosis (cf. Nonnus 40. 398), perhaps also draws on (7) (death as the beginning of new life).[82]

'In a later age what was desired was *athanasia*, a transmutation of individuality from its earthly plane to a divine plane, and this individuality was not thought to take the body with itself, but rather slough it off. For the many who were influenced by Plato a man (or at least some men) had this divine character as something inherent, which he needed only to realize; for the Orphic and Pythagorean he needed to purge it from accretions; for the adept of the mysteries he needed to win it, by rebirth or divine adoption'.[83] For the Greeks of the classical and Hellenistic era any such desire was matched by a more modest level of expectation. But as the idea spread, Heracles could more readily be deified not by preservation from the pyre but through death on the pyre itself. Heracles, unlike ordinary mortals, had a divine element, inherited from his father; and unlike ordinary heroes, who died, his divine element triumphed: he was ἥρως θεός. This is brought out in the three accounts of the process in Ovid, Seneca and Lucian (ll. cc. [n. 4]). Ovid's simile of a snake sloughing its skin recalls the 'alien cloak of flesh' which clothes the soul in Empedocles, not surprisingly, given Ovid's interest in the Pythagorean tradition.[84] In Seneca, translation to Olympus becomes absorption by the stars, with a nice ambiguity between ekpyrosis and catasterism. Lucian's Hermotimus speaks in the tradition of Plato, and points forward to the neo-Platonic interpretation of Iamblichus, where the 'meaning of the myth' finds its fullest expression.

T. C. W. STINTON
Wadham College, Oxford.

FOOTNOTES

[1] R. P. Winnington-Ingram, *Sophocles: an Interpretation* (1980) 215 and n. 33.

[2] P. E. Easterling, *ICS* 6.1, (1981) 56–72.

[3] Essays presented to Desmond Conacher, ed. M. J. Cropp (1985).

[4] Lucian, *Hermotimus* ch.7; Ovid, *Met.* 9. 250–55, 262–72; Seneca, *Herc. Oet.* 965–71; Quintus Smyrnaeus, 5.640.

[5] Theocritus, 24.82 f.; Callimachus, *hy.Cer.* 159, cf. U. von Wilamowitz, *Euripides: Herakles* I²80; Plautus, *Rudens* 766–68 and see n. 65; Cicero, *Tusc.* 2–20, cf. *Div.* 1.147 ut Herculi contigit, mortali corpore cremato in lucem animus excessit: Livy, 36.30, of M'. Acilius Glabrio in 191 sacrificing on Oeta 'where the mortal body of the god was burnt'; Pliny, *N.H.* 35.139 exusta mortalitate; Minucius Felix *Oct.* 22.7, comparison with Asclepius and with Thetis' attempt to immortalize Achilles.

[6] Iamblichus, *de Myst.* 5.12; Galen, ap. Alberuni (tr. E. C. Sachau, 1888) ii. 168.

[7] G. S. Kirk, *The nature of Greek myths* (1974) 201.

[8] See Wilamowitz (n. 5). C. Robert, *Griechische Heldensage* (1920) 597 f.; cf. K. O. Müller, *Rh.Mus.* 3 (1829) 131 = *Kleine deutsche Schriften* (1848) i. 109.

[9] Hesiod, *Th.* 950–55. fr. 25.26 ff. M.-W., fr. 229, cf. fr. 1.22. In *Od.* 11.601–4 the structure of the sentence betrays the interpolation, recognized in antiquity. Cf. M. L. West *Hesiod: Theogony* (1966) 947–55.

[10] F. Brommer, *Vasenlisten*³ (1973) 159–74, cf. 67 f. (marriage with Hebe), 100f. (Heracles with lyre).

[11] Cf. Wilamowitz (n. 5) 56.

[12] Brommer (n. 10) 188, cf. J. D. Beazley, *Etruscan vase paintings* (1947) 103–5; C. Clairmont, *AJA* 57 (1953) 85–9; Easterling (n. 2) 74 n. 29. Beazley dated the earliest *c.* 460; Professor Robertson would favour a slightly later date, say *c.* 450.

[13] For the text of these passages see n. 61 below.

[14] Hom. *hy. Cer.* 237 ff. with Richardson's note; cf. J. G. Frazer, *Apollodorus* (Loeb 1921) App. I, *Golden Bough* v. 179 ff.

[15] Minucius Felix, l.c. (n. 5); P. *O* 2. 25–26 ζώει μὲν ἐν Ὀλυμπίοις ἀποθανοῖσα βρόμῳ/κεραυνοῦ τανυέθειρα Σεμέλα; cf. E. Rohde, *Psyche* (English ed. 1925) App. I; W. Burkert, *Glotta* 39 (1961) 208–13, *Greek Religion* (1985) 198; J. Diggle, *Euripides: Phaethon* (1970) p. 178–9.

[16] Diodorus Siculus 4. 38. 4, Apollodorus 2. 7. 7. Nonnus conflates Semele's death by lightning with purification by fire. *Dion.* 8. 413–4 καὶ καθαρῷ λούσασα νέον δέμας αἴθοπι πυρσῷ/(. . .) καὶ (?) βίον ἄφθιτον ἔσχεν Ὀλύμπιον.

[17] See L. R. Farnell, *Greek hero cults* (1921) 172.

[18] Cf. P. *P.* 10. 41–2 νόσοι δ' οὔτε γῆρας οὐλόμενον κέκραται/ἱερᾷ γενεᾷ.

[19] Aëson, *Nostoi*, G. Kinkel *Epicorum Graecorum Fragmenta* (1877) 55; Jason, Simonides, *PMG* 548; the nurses of Dionysus and their husbands, Aeschylus fr. 246a R. In a later account Aeson required more sophisticated treatment, his blood being changed for a magical mixture (Ovid, *Met.* 7.285 ff.). The process could involve killing or dismemberment (Plato, *Euthydemus* 285c, Lycophron 1315, cf. Medea's deliberate failure with Pelias, and the restitution of Pelops), with a rather different symbolism. See C. Uhsadel-Gulke, *Knochen und Kessel* (1972) 26–7, J. G. Frazer, *Apollodorus* App. I for non-Greek examples. (On this topic and in n. 16, I am indebted to J. G. Howie, *PLLS* 4 (1983) 33 nn. 40, 44.)

[20] See Burkert (n. 15) 11.cc.

[21] 2.44; see Farnell (n. 17) 16–8, cf. G. R. Levy, *JHS* 54 (1934) 148.

[22] The evidence, criticized by Farnell (n. 21), is: (i) Clement *Recogn.* 10. 24 = Migne, i.1434 which may well be modelled on the Greek Heracles; (ii) Paus. 10. 4. 6, an odd story which will bear various interpretations; (iii) Menander Historicus FGH 783 F 1, on the awakening of the god, which need not suggest immolation at all (Farnell (n. 17) 168; contra Levy (n. 21)).

²³ (i) The dubious identification by Müller (n. 8) of a pyre on coins of Tarsus, and a similarly ambiguous terracotta, disputed by A. B. Cook, *Zeus* i (1914) 593 ff: H. Goldman, 'Sandon and Heracles', *Hesperia* Suppl. 8 (1949) 164 ff., who agrees with Cook that the 'pyre' is a mountain, argues that this gives a link with Heracles, but the essential link—the fire-ritual—is then wanting; (ii) Dio Chrysostom, *Or.* 33.47, who speaks of a pyre in Tarsus for 'Heracles the founder': this need not imply burning in effigy (Farnell (n. 17) 169), and might equally be modelled on the Greek Heracles; (iii) Herodian, *Hist.* 4.2. who describes in connection with the apotheosis of Roman emperors a structure like that on the coins. Burkert (n. 15) 210 accepts this evidence without comment.

²⁴ See J. G. Frazer, *Golden Bough* v. 172 ff.

²⁵ See Burkert (15) 310.

²⁶ Farnell (n. 17) 172.

²⁷ N. G. Pappadakis, *Deltion* 5 (1919) ii. 25 ff.; M. P. Nilsson, *ARW* 21 (1922) 310 ff. = *Opuscula Selecta* i (1951) 348 ff., *JHS* 43 (1923) 144 ff.; *Geschichte der griechischen Religion*² (1955) i. 131; Y. Béquignon, *La vallée du Spercheios* (1937) 204–26. On the probable Bronze Age origin, see W. Kramer, in *Helvetia antiqua*, Festschrift E. Vogt (1966) 120.

²⁸ M. P. Nilsson *JHS* (n. 27), *Griechische Feste* (1906), index s.v. Jahresfeur.

²⁹ *Σ Il.* 22.159; W. Burkert, *GRBS* 7 (1966) 117, (n. 15) 111 n. 74 (the argument was anticipated by F. Pulsen in E. Dyggve, *Das Laphriou* (1948) 352).

³⁰ Burkert (n. 15) 210.

³¹ See Wilamowitz (n. 5); M. P. Nilsson, *The Mycenean origin of Greek mythology* (1932) 201 ff.; H. A. Shapiro, *CW* 77 (1893) 11. For the wounding of Hades, cf. P. *O.* 9.28–35, with *Il.* 5.395 ff.; for the wrestling with Thanatos see A. Lesky, *Alcestis: der Mythos und das Saga* (1925); with the apples of the Hesperides and the Cerberus labour compare the analogous exploits of Gilgamesh. The prehistoric oriental analogies in which Burkert sees the remoter origin of Heracles have no bearing on the present enquiry; nor has his possible ultimate origin as a shaman in a hunting culture (*Structure and history in Greek mythology and ritual* (1979) 83–94; (n. 15) 209).

³² See Farnell (n. 17) 341 f. and ch. ix; J. N. Coldstream, JHS 96 (1976) 8–17; Burkert (n. 15) 204; refs. in T. Hadzisteliou-Price, *Historia* 22 (1973) 130 n. 7.

³³ Paus. 2.11.7, cf. M. P. Nilsson, *JHS* 43 (1923) 146.

³⁴ Hes. fr. 25.24–25; the reference of *Il.* 18.119 is unclear, though anything but a mortal's death is ruled out.

³⁵ M. L. West, *The Hesiodic Catalogue* (1985) 130; cf. his note on Hes. *Th.* 941–55.

³⁶ Cf. A. Brelich, *Gli eroi greci* (1958) 88–99; the point is well made by Shapiro (n. 31) 16.

³⁷ An example from Greek myth, as Mrs S. West reminds me, is Caeneus, made invulnerable by Poseidon, but killed by being hammered into the earth by the Centaurs; cf. Acusilaus *FGH* F 22.

³⁸ *Pace* F. Stoessl, *Der Tod des Herakles* (1945) 18 f., this does not diminish his heroism.

³⁹ Farnell (n. 17) 172; Broteas, Ovid, *Ibis* 517, Apollod. epit. 2.2; cf. E. *Andr.* 847, *HF* 1151 with Bond's note.

⁴⁰ Cf. *Il.* 2.718, *Od.* 8.219, 224; Nilsson (n. 31) 200; Kinkel (n. 19) 19, 36.

⁴¹ Cf. A. Körte, *Hermes* 39 (1894) 226 f. See also Brelich, (n. 36) 98 f., n. 69; K. Meuli, *Der griechische Agon* (1968) 58 ff.; W. Burkert, *Homo Necans* (English ed. 1984) ii.2; T. Hadzisteliou-Price in *Arktouros* (1979) 223 ff. Analogous is the festival of Asclepius (n. 44 below). The analogy is not close, since Asclepius has divine status by the time the festival is founded, but the point is that the Olympian is readily omitted in favour of a minor god.

⁴² On mountain-top sanctuaries of Zeus see M. K. Langdon, *Hesperia* Suppl. 16 (1976), esp. ch. iv.

⁴³ F. Sokolowski, *Lois sacréees des cités grecques*, (1969) 18 Γ 23.

⁴³ᵃ For other examples of a chthonic offering site ('in myth described as the grave of a hero') in the sanctuary of a god, see Burkert (n. 15) 202 and n. 41.

⁴⁴ Cf. the evidence for the festivals of Asclepius at Epidaurus (M. P. Nilsson, *Griechische Feste* (1906) 409). The great agon, Ἀπολλώνια καὶ Ἀσκληπίεια (or simply Asclepieia), attested by inscriptions from saec. iv on, was a *penteteris* (Σ P. N. 3.84), held in the sanctuary of Asclepius. But there is also earlier evidence (*IG* iv 932 2 53, 61, 65: late saec. v) for a yearly festival at Epidaurus.

⁴⁵ Thebes: Isocr. 5.32, with D. S. 4.39, cf. Nillson (n. 44) 446 and n. 3, 448 n. 7; Sicyon: Paus. 2.10.1, cf. Nilsson (n. 44) 449; Cos: *SIG*² 618. 2. 8 = *LSCG* 151 8—15: Thasos: Hdt. 1. 44, with Lloyd's note, Paus. 5. 25. 12. Cf. Burkert (n. 23) 208 and n. 3.

⁴⁶ M. Bergquist, in *Heracles on Thasos* (1973) shrewdly criticizes the French excavators' identification of the ἐσχάρα and βόθρος of the hero-cult as opposed to the βωμός of the divine cult within the sanctuary. She suggests (p. 38 ff.) that the two rituals might have been celebrated at the same altar at different times, comparing the practice at Sicyon, where the hero-offering followed the divine offering 'the next day', i.e. the same evening, possibly in the same place, Paus. 2. 10. 1, with Nilsson (n. 44) 449. Also comparable is Cos, where the same thing happened in reverse order, *inscr. cit.* n. 44, with Nilsson (n. 44) 452 f. (Bergquist's scepticism about the actual existence of a hero-cult on Thasos is at odds with the literary evidence and may be discounted: Herodotus 1.44 certainly implies it, and Paus. 5. 25. 12, which she says echoes Herodotus (p. 27) is clearly not dependent on him. Cf. K. Clinton in *AJA* 79 (1975) 384, J. M. Cook in *CR* 26 (1976) 292.)

⁴⁷ Burkert (n. 41) I. 1., cf. *GRBS* 7 (1966) 103 n. 36, (n. 23) 203; see also n. 43a above.

⁴⁸ Asclepius' punishment by Zeus is mentioned in Hesiod's catalogue (fr. 50 MW) and serves as an exemplum in P. *P.* 3.54-60, A. *Ag*, 1022-4; but 'the evidence of the later historic period (sc. saec. v on) leaves us in no doubt that (he) was worshipped as a full-blown θεός' (Farnell (n. 17) 234). Amphiaraus and his chariot were swallowed by the earth (S. *El.* 837 ff., cf. Paus. 1.34.2), but he was worshipped as a god 'first in Oropus and later by all the Greeks' (Paus. l.c.; cf. the claim that Heracles was worshipped as a god first in Attica, D. S. 4. 39). On the nature of the dual aspect of Asclepius and Amphiaraus—hero promoted to god—see Farnell (n. 17) ch. x and p. 58 ff., 406.

⁴⁹ It is because of these alternatives in Greek myth that the passion of Christ, who is often compared with Heracles from antiquity onwards (cf. M. Simon, *Heracles et Christianisme* (1955) esp. ch. ii; A. Toynbee, *A Study of History* vi (1939) 465-76), can never, for the Christian hearing it reenacted in the Gospel narrative, in which the resurrection inevitably succeeds it, have the tragic finality that Heracles' death would have for Sophocles' audience. This is not to say that their knowledge of his divinity in cult would not modify their response to the play; it might by contrast, for example, sharpen their awareness that the *Trachiniae* does *not* end in apotheosis, and so diverges from the familiar alternative (cf. Stinton (n. 3)).

⁵⁰ Cf. Beazley (note 12) 104.

⁵¹ *ARV*² 238, early saec. v; *Bacchylides* 3. 37-62, cf. Hdt. 1. 86.

⁵² Certainly earlier than that of Herodotus, which is adjusted to suit the requirements of its context.

⁵³ Beazley (n. 12) 104-5; cf. A. B. Cook, *Zeus* iii (1940).

⁵⁴ Cf. Langdon (n. 42) 7, 79-81; A. B. Cook, *Zeus* i (1914).

⁵⁵ As is suggested by Mrs S. West, *CQ* 34 (1984) 295 n. 14. The extinction of Heracles' pyre could not of course be modelled on Euripides without a most implausibly tight chronology.

⁵⁶ On A. fr. 73 GR, the only surviving fragment, see H. Lloyd-Jones, H. Weir

Smyth, *Aeschylus* (Loeb 1957) ii. ²586–90. Lloyd-Jones cautiously favours the interpretation of Zielinski, followed by Srebrny, that the fragment best fits a plot like that of the *Trachiniae*. The supplement in C.3 seems unavoidable, so the lines are spoken by Heracles. As restored by Lloyd-Jones after Srebrny, the passage is in the past tense; thus presumably a reported speech of Heracles on the pyre, perhaps addressed to Philoctetes. A reported speech might conceivably occur in a play with a quite different plot; e.g. that of Euripides' *Heraclidae*: but it most obviously fits a play dealing with the events before Heracles' death. Other supplements, however, give a future reference, e.g.:

> πυρὰ]ν γὰρ αὐτότευκ[τον] ἥν εν[τέλλομαι
> Οἴτη]σ ἐν ὑψηλοῖσι θα[μν]ουχοι[σ κτίσαι,
> εἰς τῇ]νδε παῖδες οἵδε [μ᾽α]μφιμήτορες
> οἴσουσι]ν ἄρδην καυσίμοις ἐν δ[ενδρεσιν
> οἰδοῦν]τα καὶ λοπῶντα φαρμάκου [μένει.

1 end, 2 end, 4 beginning *exempli gratia* Stinton. Heracles will then be instructing his sons to build his pyre, as Dio Chrysostom says he does (*Or.* 78; cf. T. Zielinski, *Tragodumenon libri tres* (1925) 87 just as he instructs Hyllus in the *Trachiniae*. αὐτότευκτον will in any case mean not 'ready-made', 'natural', but 'built by your own hands'(so Srebrny, *Eos* 45 (1951) 41 ff.); cf. *Trach.* 1194 αὐτόχειρα in the corresponding context.

⁵⁷ To the fragmentary vases noted in n. 12 add a recently-published Attic red-figured *psykter* of the mid-fifth century ('460–450'), which shows Heracles sitting on the pyre and giving his bow to Philoctetes, with no sign of apotheosis, a unique representation (J. R. Guy, *Images de céramiques*, Publ. de l'univ. de Rouen 96 (1983) 152–3; I owe this reference to Professor Boardman). The absence of apotheosis may simply be due to the restricted shape of the ground.

⁵⁸ Paus. 9. 3. 8, cf. Nilsson (n. 44) 51.

⁵⁹ W. Burkert, *MH* 29 (1972) 84. It is noteworthy that the only extant epic accounts of Heracles' death through the robe and subsequent apotheosis, those in Hesiod's *Catalogue* (fr. 25. 20 ff., explicit; fr. 229, implicit; cf. West (n. 35) 112), omit the pyre. The omission is conceivably due to the very summary narrative characteristic of this work (cf. West, n. 35) 3).

⁶⁰ This does not mean that their awareness of Heracles' divinity in cult would be irrelevant to their response to the play; see n. 49 above.

⁶¹ E. l.c. ἔστιν ἐν οὐρανῷ βεβα/κὼς τεὸς γόνος, ὦ γεραιέ/ά· φεύγει λόγον ὡς τὸν Ἀι/δα δόμον κατέβα, πυρός/ δεινᾷ φλογὶ σῶμα δαισθείς. For my translation see T. Zielinski, *Philologus* 9 (1896) 493 f.; cf. Stinton (n. 3), S. l.c. ἵν᾽ ὁ χάλκασπις ἀνὴρ θεοῖς/ πλάθει ⁺πᾶσιν⁺ θείῳ πυρὶ παμφαής,/ Οἴτας ὑπὲρ ὄχθων. Cf. C. W. Müller 'Gleiches zu Gleichem' *Klass. Phil. Studien* 31 (1965) 167–73, and see n. 77 below. Jebb suggests that the fire was lightning (cf. C. M. Edsman, *Ignis divinus* (1949) 234, but this belongs to a later assimilation with Asclepius, etc., mentioned above.

⁶² P. *I.* 4. 71–72 τοῖσιν ἐν δυθμαῖσιν αὐγᾶν/ φλὸξ ἀνατελλομένα συνεχὲς παννυχίζει,/ αἰθέρα κνισάεντι λακτίζοισα καπνῷ. Cf. Nilsson (n. 44) 466 f.

⁶³ Theocr. 24. 82–83 δώδεκά οἱ τελέσαντι πεπρωμένον ἐν Διὸς οἰκεῖν/ μόχθους, θνητὰ δὲ πάντα πυρὰ τραχίνιος ἕξει. Callim. *h. Dian.* 159 φρυγίη περ ὑπὸ δρυὶ γυῖα θεωθείς, Cf. Wilamowitz, (n. 5) Φρυγία ὄρυς Τραχῖνος, ἔνθα ἔκαη ὁ Ἡρακλῆς Σ (cf. *EM* 465.31 'every wooded mountain is called Ida').

⁶⁴ A. R. 4. 869–70 ἡ μὲν γὰρ βροτέας αἰεὶ περὶ σάρκας ἔδαιεν/ νύκτα διὰ μέσσην φλογμῷ πυρός. Cf. N. J. Richardson (ed.), *The Homeric Hymn to Demeter* (1974) 237. With the language here cf. Apollod. 3. 13. 6 εἰς τὸ πῦρ ἐγκρύβουσα τῆς νυκτὸς ἔφθειρεν ὃ ἦν αὐτῷ θνητὸν πατρῷον, of Thetis and Achilles; ib. 1. 5. 1 τὰς νύκτας εἰς πῦρ κατετίθει τὸ βρέφος καὶ περιῄρει τὰς θνητὰς σάρκας αὐτοῦ, of Demeter and Demophon; Plutarch, *Isis* 16 (357a) νύκτωρ δὲ περικαίειν τὰ θνητὰ τοῦ σώματος . . . ἄχρι οὗ τὴν βασίλισσαν . . . ὡς εἶδε

περικαιόμενον τὸ βρέφος, ἀφελέσθαι τὴν ἀθανασίαν αὐτοῦ, of Isis and the son of Byblos. These passages might conceivably illuminate the title of Spintharos of Heracles' tragedy Ἡρακλῆς περικαιόμενος and the parody, if it is one, of Strattis, Ζώπυρος περικαιόμενος (cf. E. G. Turner on *P. Oxy.* 2454, T. B. L. Webster, *Studies in later Greek comedy* (1953) 29, 135). This would make the burning away of Heracles' mortal part a familiar idea in early saec. iv. But περικαιόμενος may just mean 'scorched', as it is usually rendered.

⁶⁵ 'ignem magnum hic faciam.'—'quin inhumanum exuras tibi?' Cf. A. E. Housman, *CR* 32 (1918) 162 f. = *Classical papers* (1972) iii. 960 f.

⁶⁶ Rohde (n. 15) 21; *Rigveda* compared, n. 40; stories of Achilles, Demeter and Demophon to be so explained, n. 41 cited by R. C. T. Parker, *Miasma* (1983) 227 n. 111: 'the funeral fire, of course, purged of the impurity of mortality'. (Dr Parker agrees, however, that the annulment of pollution caused by death is not the same as the annulment of mortality, either here or in Archilochus, l.c. below). Burkert (n. 15) 134 describes Demeter as putting Demophon on the fire 'um es "von allem Sterblichen zu reinigen"', the quoted words being presumably adapted from Apollod. 1. 5. 1, (n. 64). Richardson (n. 64) 234), *à propos* of Demophon, speaks of 'Melikertes "immortalized in the cauldron"', a conflation of (1) Apollod. 3.4.3, where Ino kills by boiling him in a cauldron; (2) Σ Arg. P. *I.* (p.192. 5–10 Dr.), where Athamas kills the brother Learchos, and Ino puts him in a cauldron of hot water before going mad, presumably to restore him, like Pelops (cf. n. 19). (3) W. Dittenberger, *OGI* 611, a dedication from Syria on behalf of Trajan's safety to Leukothea (= Ino) by the nephew of one ἀποθεωθέντος ἐν τῷ λέβητι δι' οὗ αἱ ἑορταὶ ἄγονται 'apotheosised in the cauldron used for the ritual of the festivals' (so L. R. Farnell, *JHS* 36 (1916) 42. Cf. *GHC* 42–43. A. Lesky in *R–E* 15. 515, Richardson (n. 64) 247), i.e. of an initiate in the (late) mystery cult of Ino-Leucothea. Farnell and Lesky inferred that this was the original meaning of the myth, which begs the question I am raising. (Dr. Richardson is not now inclined to regard Melikertes as relevant to his argument.)

⁶⁷ Archilochus fr. 9. 10–11c, εἰ κείνου κεφαλὴν καὶ χαρίεντα μέλεα/ Ἥφαιστος καθαροῖσιν ἐν εἵμασιν ἀμφεπονήθη ... See D. C. Kurtz and J. Boardman, *Greek burial customs* (1971) 142 ff., 149 ff., 200 ff.; cf. n. 72 below. Emped. B. 126 σαρκῶν ἀλλογνῶτι ... χιτῶνι.

⁶⁸ E. l.c. ἵν' αὐτῶν σώμαθ' ἡγνίσθη πυρί Kaibel 104, cf. Callim. (n. 63) and possibly A.P. 7.123.

⁶⁹ Richardson (n. 64) 22 f., 211 f., 232; G. E. Mylonas, *Eleusis and the Eleusinian mysteries* (1962) 205 ff., figs. 83, 84; comparison with Proetids, Burkert (n. 15) 137 (cf. also the purification of sacrificial victims with a torch, found already in Babylonian practice) (n. 41). A similar purification, usually compared with that of Heracles, is depicted on a saec. v Attic relief, in which a child is seated on the ground while one of two women points a torch at him; Demeter is also present. Burkert's comment, 'apotheosis by fire seems to be indicated' (n. 23) 288 is quite unjustified. See Richardson (n. 64) 23 f., 232 f.; picture, M. P. Nilsson, *Geschichte der griechische Religion²* (1950) pl. 44. 2, cf. *ARW* 34 (1937) 108 ff. and Pl. I = *Opera Selecta* ii (1952) 624 ff., where Nilsson proposes the interpretation followed by Burkert.

⁷⁰ Burkert (n. 47); Richardson (n. 64) 234. *Pace* Burkert (n. 15) with n. 40), the protection against the underworld given to Heracles by the mysteries is not to the point.

⁷¹ On Persian and Indian doctrine see M. L. West, *Early Greek philosophy and the Orient* (1971) 178.

⁷² Cf. Burkert (n. 15) 191, with refs. in n. 7: add R. M. Cook, *Antiquity* (1960) 178.

⁷³ I use E. R. Dodds' term 'shaman' (*The Greeks and the Irrational* (1951), 144 f.) without endorsing his thesis that these Greek figures derived from Siberian shamans. Cf. Burkert (n. 15) 195 and n. 38.

⁷⁴ Hdt. 2.123; cf. Burkert, l.c.

⁷⁵ E. fr. 835 cf. fr. 638; first in Heraclitus, frr. 62, 68; see Dodds (n. 73) 152.

⁷⁶ Joh. 12. 24, I. Cor. 15. 36, cf. Epictetus 2. 6. 13; E. *Hyps.* fr. 60. 90–96B, Aesch. *Cho.* 127–8. On Eleusinian belief see Richardson (n. 64) 14–16, W. K. C. Guthrie, *The Greeks and their Gods* (1950) 280; Nilsson (n. 69) 1.675; Burkert (n. 15) 432.

⁷⁷ Kaibel 21 = Peek 20, attributed to Euripides by U. von Wilamowitz, *Hellenistische Dichtung* (1921) i. 125. Cf., e.g. *Suppl.* 531–6, 1140, *Hel.* 1015–16, frr. 195, 839, 908b, S. 971, *Hyps.* (n. 76); Guthrie, (n. 76) 262 ff., Müller, (n. 61), Collard on *Suppl.* 531–36, Kannicht on *Hel.* l.c.; cf. also A. *Cho.* 127, Epicharmus #9, Xenophanes A 1.27 f.

⁷⁸ Evidence given in Peek, 1754–84 (saec. iv-iii); ib. 595 (after mid-saec. iv). Before 350: ib. 1755.

⁷⁹ *Od.* 11.218–22, cit. Rohde, (n. 66) p. 49, n. 38; cf. *Il.* 23. 75 f.

⁸⁰ Plat.*Crat.* 400d, *Gorg.* 493a; probably Pythagorean, see Dodds (n. 73). Cf. Empedocles 13.126 (n. 67).

⁸¹ R. Lattimore, *Themes in Greek and Latin epitaphs* (1942) 24; Cf. Rohde (n. 66) p. 461, n. 150; Chrysippus, fr. 499 R.-P.

⁸² Edsmann (n. 61) 202 f.; Nonnus, l.c.

⁸³ A. D. Nock, 'Cremation and burial in the Roman empire' *HTR* 25 (1932) 353 = *Essays on religion and the ancient world* (1972) i. 303.

⁸⁴ Ovid *Met.* 9.266–70, after Virg. *Aen.* 2.470–5.

Euripides' Alkestis: *five aspects of an interpretation*

This article is intended to be a contribution towards an overall understanding of *Alkestis*. I discuss five topics which seem to me to be of major importance for our interpretation of the play. Whereas many previous treatments have concentrated on matters of characterization, especially relating to Admetos, the emphasis of my own account will be different. Only the fourth of my sections will engage with the debate over character. For the rest, I shall be analysing the changing significance of the door in the visual stage action (section 1), the boundary between life and death (section 2), the role of Herakles (section 3), and the tone of the work as a whole (section 5).

1. *The door of the house*
The *skene* represents Admetos' palace at Pherai. In the centre is the door, the visual focus for most of the significant actions in the plot.

According to a stage direction in some manuscripts, the play begins with the emergence of Apollo from the house. While it is impossible to demonstrate the correctness of such a direction, it is surely incontrovertible that such a beginning is symbolically appropriate. Apollo's identification with the fortunes of Admetos is now over: the presence of the god from above is to be replaced by that of the god from below. Thus at the end of the first scene, Apollo leaves by the side exit, but Thanatos enters the palace through the central doorway.[1]

When the chorus arrive they notice (98 ff.) that outside the door there is no sign either of hair cut in mourning or of a vessel of water—needed, after a death, so that those emerging can purify themselves before resuming contact with normality outside.[2] The reason for these absences is of course that Alkestis is still alive. When she has emerged, spoken and died, she is carried back into the house; and the house-door then takes on the significance which had been prefigured as Thanatos passed through it: it becomes the point of transition between the polluted interior and the non-polluted world outside.

With the arrival of Herakles on his way north, the door's significance is intensified. In order to treat Herakles properly, i.e. as a ξένος and φίλος should treat his ξένος and φίλος, Admetos must persuade him to enter the house—in spite of the evidence from Admetos' appearance that this is a place of mourning. (Incidentally, it is surely quite likely that a vessel of water *has* now been placed on stage outside the door.) The pivot of Admetos' persuasion of Herakles is linguistic: the woman who has died was ὀθνεῖος, 'no blood relation' (532–3).[3] For the first of two occasions in the play, a man gets his φίλος to enter the house by deception, but for the best of motives.

After the carrying-out of Alkestis and the argument with Pheres, the next scene, between Herakles and the servant, goes back to the linguistic point which I have just mentioned, but with a different word in question. 'Why so gloomy?', asks Herakles; 'the πῆμα is θυραῖον' (778); 'the woman who died was θυραῖος' (805). 'She was only too θυραῖος', replies the servant (811). Herakles: 'These don't sound like θυραῖα πήματα' (814); and later, when he knows the true identity of the deceased: 'He persuaded me by saying it was a θυραῖον κῆδος he was taking to the tomb' (828). θυραῖος—etymologically, 'at, connected with, the door' (hence Hermes, that quintessential boundary-crosser, can be Hermes Thuraios).[4] But just as 'Go and see who's at the door' means 'Go and see who's *outside* the door', so θυραῖος can mean 'one connected with the outside', 'an outsider'.[5] And a wife is an 'outsider', brought across the threshold into the husband's house from outside.

It is exactly this reference which becomes poignantly explicit in the next scene. Admetos, having just buried Alkestis, returns to confront the house-door, now hateful to him because of yet another range of associations which the door has.

> ἰώ, στυγναὶ
> πρόσοδοι, στυγναὶ δ᾽ ὄψεις χήρων
> μελάθρων . . .   (861 ff.)
> ὦ σχῆμα δόμων, πῶς εἰσέλθω;   (911)

He is reminded of that other time when he passed through the house-door, when he and Alkestis, white-robed instead of black, surrounded not by lamentation but by marriage songs, together entered the house, with Admetos holding her hand—that is, her wrist—in his (917).[6]

As the door was a boundary-marker in the case of a death, so it was in the case of a wedding. A Greek wedding dramatized in ritual terms the transition of a woman from the οἶκος of her father to the οἶκος, or more specifically the bedroom, of her husband. The crossing of the threshold of the new οἶκος was one aspect of this transition. There was, as far as I know, nothing comparable to the Roman custom[7] of carrying the bride over the threshold (so marking the danger and significance of the passage); and the door of the θάλαμος or bridal chamber seems if anything to have been of more importance (it was outside *that* door that a θυρωρός was posted);[8] nevertheless, the crossing of the threshold of the house itself *was* marked in Greece, since it was there that the couple were welcomed by the groom's parents.[9]

Recalling his marriage, Admetos describes his present dilemma:

πῶς γὰρ δόμων τῶνδ᾽ εἰσόδους ἀνέξομαι;   (941)
ἡ μὲν γὰρ ἔνδον ἐξελᾷ μ᾽ ἐρημία   (944)

ἔξωθεν δέ (950): 'But outside' there will be weddings, social gatherings of women of Alkestis' age—and that too will be intolerable. Apollo's unique gift to him has resulted in a unique dilemma.

But when all is said and done, *Alkestis* is not a tragedy, it is a non-satyric fourth play. And so we have the scene where Herakles returns with a veiled woman (see section 2). He reproaches Admetos for entertaining him as if concerned only for θυραίου πήματος (1014—a line unnecessarily deleted by Méridier following Lachmann) and he urges Admetos to take the woman into the house. When Admetos at last relents, Herakles goes further: Admetos must lead her in *with his own right hand*—enacting, of course, the entry of a bridal couple (1115). For the second time a φίλος is deceiving a φίλος in order to be kind—although there is in this case perhaps a fine balance between our sense of the pain of the deceived φίλος and our anticipation of his joy. But eventually Admetos looks at Alkestis' face; and what came perilously close to being a bitter parody of part of a wedding ceremony turns into a resolemnization of the union which only death has put asunder. From the beginning of the play the significance of the action of entering the house has varied as the house itself has successively become a place of death, hospitality, mourning, and marriage. At the end, the restored stability of the house is sealed by a definitive re-entry of Admetos and Alkestis over the threshold, as man and wife.

2. *Life and death*

The relations between life and death in *Alkestis* are complex;[10] and perhaps the most interesting aspect of this complexity is the fact that, for virtually the whole of the play, Alkestis herself is presented as being between life and death. Before going inside the house, Thanatos says that the person whose hair his sword has 'consecrated' (ἁγνίσῃ, 76) by cutting it is thenceforth ἱερός to the gods below: so begins Alkestis' separation from life. In practically their first words the chorus express doubt about whether Alkestis is alive or dead (80 ff.). When a servant-girl comes out of the house, and the chorus ask her, 'Is she alive or dead?', they are told:

$$\text{καὶ ζῶσαν εἰπεῖν καὶ θανοῦσαν ἔστι σοι} \quad (141)$$

By her actions—washing herself as a preliminary to putting on the clothes in which she will die; praying to the Hearth and adorning the altars of the other gods; bidding farewell to her bed, children and servants—Alkestis shows that she is in the process of dying. It is not a physiological, 'Hippokratean' process ('seventh day: great chill; acute fever; much sweat; death'); rather it is a social process, involving severance from all the cultural ties which bind a person to life.[11] The counterpart to the social process of dying is the belief that death is not instantaneous, but a journey: so Alkestis sees a two-oared boat, and Charon calls, τί μέλλεις; (252, 255). The reference to Charon is significant: he, like Thanatos,[12] is an *intermediate* agent of death. Perhaps this makes the ultimate rescue more imaginatively credible: the dead woman has not yet been definitively incarcerated in Hades. Furthermore, although she dies at line 391, Alkestis in a way remains, even after that, between life and death. We have already been told (348 ff.) of Admetos' plan to give his wife a kind of continued existence by creating a life-like statue of her; and when Herakles arrives and asks, 'How is your wife?', Admetos' reply ἔστιν τε κοὐκέτ' ἔστιν (521) seems to perpetuate in a linguistic manner this ambiguity of Alkestis' status. And even at the very end of the play, when Death has been defeated, Alkestis is still not yet fully alive. As throughout the play, so at its end, she is poised on the boundary between life and death. To see how this can be so, it will be necessary to explore two themes: veiling and silence.

On the evidence of Admetos' words at 1050 ('She is young, *to judge from her clothing and appearance*') the scholiast inferred that Alkestis was veiled; and he was surely right. At 1121 Herakles instructs Admetos: βλέψον πρὸς αὐτήν—and here Herakles will have unveiled her. (Compare *Herakles Mainomenos* 1227, where Theseus, unveiling Herakles, tells him: βλέψον πρὸς ἡμᾶς.) The veil in *Alkestis* is powerful from the sheerly dramatic point of view, in that it makes possible the tense persuasion of Admetos by Herakles, which depends on Admetos' inability correctly to identify a woman—just as Admetos earlier persuaded Herakles when Herakles failed correctly to identify a woman.

But there is more to veiling than that. A veil often marks out an

individual who is in a marginal or transitional state. Those in
mourning veiled themselves.[13] Those in the abnormal state of being
polluted might cover their heads.[14] And of course veiling might mark
a transition with quite different emotional resonances: as Kassandra
says in *Agamemnon*, 'My oracle will no longer peep out from a veil like
a newly-married bride' (1178–9). That the bridal veil signals a
transition is evident enough; but there is uncertainty over details. We
know that the bride was veiled at the meal at her father's house,[15] but
when did she *un*veil? In his recent account of the Anakalupteria or
Ceremony of Unveiling, Oakley[16] followed Deubner[17] in placing it at
the house of the bride's father, i.e. *before* the procession to the new
house. However, not only is it more plausible on general grounds of
ritual symbolism that the bride made the transition from house to
house veiled,[18] but there is a considerable number of vases showing
the bride in the bridal procession with her head still veiled, even if her
face is visible.[19] Whenever the unveiling took place, it is clear that the
moment when the groom saw the bride's face was an important one in
the wedding ritual (one name for the gifts presented to the bride at the
Anakalupteria was ὀπτήρια, 'to do with seeing');[20] and realizing the
importance of the moment of seeing the bride may sharpen our
awareness of what is at stake in the unveiling in Euripides' play.

What, then, of the veiled Alkestis? She is in a doubly transitional
state. Firstly, she is still between death and life, between the other
world and this.[21] Secondly, her new arrival at Admetos' οἶκος is like
the prelude to a second marriage. There is no reason to believe that
Alkestis' unveiling *before entering the house* represents a direct transcrip-
tion of wedding ritual. Rather it would seem that the symbolism of
unveiling is borrowed and adapted to fit the specific dramatic
requirements of the play. Alkestis must unveil on stage (i.e. outside
the house) because Admetos must recognize her on stage.

I have repeatedly spoken of Alkestis as a character poised between
life and death. It remains to consider one last aspect of this point.
'You may speak to her', Herakles tells Admetos, 'but it is not yet
themis for you to hear her addressing you, until she has been
deconsecrated from the gods below, when the third dawn comes'
(1132; 1144–6). The connection between silence, covering the head,
and real or symbolic death is not unfamiliar to us. We think perhaps
of Benedictine monks, who wear the hood over the head at all times
when forbidden to speak; but when they take their final vows, they lie
still and prostrate on a pall (not only physically resembling the dead
but explicitly 'dying to the world') and have the hood pinned under
the chin; they must then keep silence until the hood is unpinned—at
Communion, on the third day afterwards.[22] From ancient Greece we

have several examples of a congruence between veiling and silence. Aischylos' Niobe sits veiled and silent until the third day;[23] and his Achilles seems to have covered his head and been silent in both *Phrygians* and *Myrmidons*—his silence persisting in the latter case, apparently, till the third day.[24] Euripides' Phaidra is veiled and silent at one point in *Hippolytos* through shame at her polluting state; and it is her third day without food.[25] In *Alkestis* the congruence is only partial: the silence persists for three days *after* the unveiling. This is partly a matter of dramatic necessity: as we observed earlier, she *has* to unveil, but there is no compelling reason for her to speak. But her silence is appropriate in ritual terms too, since it marks her unusually anomalous condition. The words of a person in any state of pollution might be harmful to others: as Orestes says in *Eumenides*, 'the law is that the murderer be ἄφθογγος until purified'.[26] But this applies *a fortiori* to Alkestis: she has died and been buried. Plutarch notes that anyone for whom carrying-out and burial had been performed, as though he were dead, was considered impure by the Greeks, and they would not let such a person associate with themselves or approach a temple; and Hesychios refers to a ceremony of reenacted birth designed to admit the δευτερόποτμος back to life.[27] Did a symbolic silence figure in the ritual for managing such a rare and anomalous case, and was Euripides adapting that silence in *Alkestis*? There is, I think, no evidence; and the silence could just as easily have been Euripidean invention, appropriate because of Alkestis' still-dangerous link with the dead. Or could he, here too, have been borrowing from the wedding ritual? When the bride was veiled before the Anakalup-teria, did she also have to keep silent, being restored to normal communication only after the unveiling? According to Pollux, an alternative name for the Anakalupteria gifts was προσφθεγκτήρια, 'gifts of salutation'.[28] In any case, we would be dealing, not with a simple 'reflection' of ritual, but with its adaptation to the needs of a given dramatic context.

Even at the end, then, Alkestis is not yet fully alive. Through her fate, the relation between life and death is shown to be in certain respects ambiguous. Now closely related to this ambiguity is what seems to be an outright paradox. The plot is based on the assumption that Death will inevitably get what is due to him: if Admetos does not die, someone else must. Futhermore, there is in the course of the work a series of references to the *fixity* of the boundary between life and death: (*a*) the fate of Asklepios (3–4, 122 ff.; *cf.* 970) who raised the dead and was thunderbolted for it; (*b*) the emphatic words of Herakles at 528 ('Most people reckon there is a big difference between being alive and being dead'); (*c*) the attitude of the chorus:

'There is no way round Necessity' (962 ff.), 'You will not raise the dead' (985–6).[29] And yet *Alkestis* ends with the defeat of Thanatos and the restoration of Alkestis. Is the boundary between life and death not, then, fixed, as we have been led to believe? On this paradox two things should be said.

First we must consider who it is that is apparently threatening the boundary between life and death. Of all the figures in Greek myth, Herakles is the one who seems to be licensed most regularly to push beyond boundaries. In particular, he breaks the confines of mortality in two ways: downwardly, by invading Hades and stealing Kerberos; and upwardly, by achieving acceptance into Olympos. In *Alkestis* the boundary between life and death is not abolished or redrawn: 'after' the action of the play, things will remain as they are. It is just that, in one exceptional case, the exceptional hero *par excellence* is able to intervene and postpone (but not, we imagine, cancel) the death of Alkestis.

This leads us to the second point. In the house of Admetos, normal life has at last, we must assume, been reestablished. Normal life—and normal death: the recent suspension of normal relationships between life and death has, presumably, come to an end. From the beginning of the play, the relationship between life and death has been in an unusual state, with both the main characters poised in different ways between the two; finally, the usual distance between the extremes is restored.[30] Perhaps one respect in which *Alkestis* asserts itself as a 'fourth play' rather than a tragedy is that, at its conclusion, at least one ambiguity is resolved instead of being left open-ended.

3. *Herakles*

In order to appreciate Herakles' role in *Alkestis* it will be useful first to remind ourselves about his place within Greek mythology as a whole, and the literary tradition in particular.[31]

Herakles was the great 'helper' to whom one could appeal in time of trouble. Myths about him range widely: from the East to the far West, from (as we mentioned) the underworld to Olympos. In other ways too he is associated with the limits of humanity: he is repeatedly connected with animals, which he kills or controls; he has to deal with centaurs (incompletely human) and with Amazons (abnormally human). Sometimes, it is true, Herakles is situated in the social rather than the natural world, as when he sacks the cities of Troy and Oichalia. But here once more he is hardly a comfortably socialized being: he is a disrupter of civilization, a hero whose boundless violence can be a potential threat to order as well as (when he slays monsters) a supporter of it.

Literary representations of the hero are heterogeneous. It will be convenient to take three examples.

(a) Praise-poetry. In Pindar Herakles has an honoured place as a representative of athleticism, of ἀρετή, and of a willingness to strive in order to deserve the reward of victory. In return for his exertions he attained peace and rest on Olympos, with Hebe by his side (*Nem.* 1. 69 ff.). Such ambivalence as there is in the Pindaric Herakles[32] fades before the presentation of the hero as a shining example to emulate.

(b) Tragedy. Here Herakles is a much more paradoxical and ambiguous figure. In *Trachiniai*, for instance, he is the monster-slayer who is himself a monster, the mighty hero who is brought so low as to be subservient to the weak (Omphale, Deianira): in *Herakles Mainomenos* he is the hero who is both son of a god and son of a man. In general tragedy explores the darker and more problematic side of Herakles—he is a defender of civilization, yet he can kill his own wife and children, and is only just prevented from killing his father.

(c) Comedy. Once more, of course, we have a different emphasis. Athenaios (411a) gives us a picture of the gluttonous Herakles: 'Epicharmos, for example, says in his *Busiris*: "First, if you should see him eating, you would die. His gullet thunders inside, his jaw rattles, his molar crackles, his canine gnashes, he sizzles at the nostrils, and he waggles his ears." '[33] And in Ion's satyr-play *Omphale* the audience heard that 'not content with the steaks, he ate the charcoal from the grill as well' (Athen. 411b).

Where do we locate *Alkestis* in all this? The Herakles of this play combines the three types which we have reviewed. The mighty athlete praised by Pindar is the heroic figure who strides boldly out to wrestle with Death. The fact that it is *with Death* that Herakles fights reminds us of the tragic Herakles, whose exploits so often have the profoundest implications for humanity and for the boundary between life and death. And the scene in which the bewildered servant reports the drunken misbehaviour of his unruly guest reminds us of the Herakles of comedy. But it is important that we do not misrepresent the balance between the three aspects of Herakles in *Alkestis*. In particular, we must realize that there is nothing tragic about Herakles' own position. He is on his way to Thrace to perform one of his labours; that is, he is *in the middle* of his labours. His situation is therefore unproblematic: only when his labours are over, as in *Herakles Mainomenos*, will his fate become precarious. In *Alkestis* he is merely in transit. The only tragic or near-tragic events with which he comes into contact are events in the life of the Thessalian household in which he is entertained.

One other question is worth asking before we leave Herakles: why is he not polluted either by entering the house of Admetos when the corpse is still inside, or by his wrestling match with Death? On the first point, no one in the play expresses any criticism of Admetos for exposing Herakles to possible pollution, so we can only conclude that no such pollution was felt to have been incurred—presumably because pollution most strongly affected the deceased's immediate kin, a group to which Herakles clearly did not belong.[34] As for the second point, I suggest that the reason why Apollo (like Artemis in *Hippolytos*) feels compelled to avoid a house where Death is present, while Herakles can go so far as to wrestle with Death, is that, in religious terms, the distance between Apollo and Death is greater than that between Herakles and Death: Apollo is a god of the above, Death a god of the below, and Herakles a figure whose activities span both spheres. With a splendidly structuralist logic, Herakles can operate where Apollo fears to tread.

4. *Admetos and hospitality*

The issue of how we are to take the character of Admetos has come virtually to dominate criticism of the play. On the one hand there are scholars who detect numerous hints that Admetos' willingness to accept his wife's sacrifice is represented by Euripides in a negative light.[35] On the other hand there are those who prefer a 'naïve' reading, accepting the lines at face value rather than looking between and behind them. My own view coincides with the latter approach, and in particular with the excellent discussion by Burnett.[36] I shall confine myself here to some specific comments in support of a 'non-ironical' reading of *Alkestis*.

A small but significant detail occurs in the scene where the servant tells the chorus about Alkestis' moving farewell to her children, marriage bed and household slaves. Although the chorus are full of praise for Alkestis (150–1), they express sympathy for Admetos too:

$$\mathring{\omega} \ \tau\lambda\tilde{\eta}\mu o\nu, \ o\mathring{\iota}as \ o\mathring{\iota}os \ \mathring{\omega}\nu \ \mathring{\alpha}\mu\alpha\rho\tau\acute{\alpha}\nu\epsilon\iota s \qquad (144)$$

It would have been perfectly possible for Euripides to have written a play in which Admetos appeared as unpleasantly insensitive as is Jason in *Medea*; but that is not what he has done. Again, nothing in the farewell scene between husband and wife can lead us to regard Admetos as a hypocrite, or to regard his grief as insincere. As a result of his generosity to a god, he has been given a gift; and the gifts of the gods, as Paris reminded Hektor (*Il.* iii 65), are not to be cast away. Apollo's gift to Admetos was life; and one of the play's paradoxes is that this 'life' is no life at all without the person who made the life possible. But, for most of *Alkestis*, the result of the paradox is sympathy for Admetos, not censure of him. For most of *Alkestis* the question, 'What do we make of a man who allows his wife to die so that he himself may live?' is simply not asked, because that is not what the play is mainly about.

The positive presentation of Admetos is maintained in the episode where he deceives Herakles into accepting hospitality. How are we to evaluate his decision to withhold the truth because he does not wish to fail in his obligations as a ξένος? Euripides does not present it as absurd or foolish. On the contrary, it is—as Herakles himself later recognizes (855 ff.)—the act of a noble man and a true friend. In a society such as that of ancient Greece, where travellers were bereft of all the social ties which made existence practicable when they were at home, the institution of ξενία was of enormous practical and emotional significance. Hence it was sanctioned by Zeus (Xenios) himself; and its obligations could be ignored only at great peril: in myth, those who break ξενία invariably suffer for it, whether they are behaving as a wicked host in their own house (Tantalos) or as a wicked guest in the house of another (Paris). In presenting Admetos as a good ξένος Euripides was reflecting a fundamental custom of Greek society; although the chorus is at first critical of Admetos, his explanation— he absolutely refuses to turn away a friend—convinces them, and they sing an ode in praise of his nobility.

Then, with a sharp contrast so typical of Euripides, we have the bitter scene between Admetos and Pheres. Now *for the first time* Euripides confronts us with the moral issue implicit in the starting-point of the plot, namely: what do we make of a man who allows his wife to die so that he himself may live? So far we have seen Admetos only as loving husband and noble host; now suddenly we are forced to look at the other side of the coin—to see him as a murderer:

> σὺ γοῦν ἀναιδῶς διεμάχου τὸ μὴ θανεῖν,
> καὶ ζῇς παρελθὼν τὴν πεπρωμένην τύχην,
> ταύτην κατακτάς·   (694–6)

Whether this scene can outweigh the positive evaluation of Admetos which the play has given us so far is perhaps something which each individual reader or spectator must answer for him-/herself; in my own view it certainly does not. The scene makes Admetos more complex, and therefore more interesting. We see his grief take a new direction, leading him to be fiercely aggressive to his own father. Hence his isolation becomes even more complete. The ground is thus prepared for the truly distressing scene at 861 ff. when Admetos, returning after the funeral, comes face to face with the empty house. Here once more, as in the early part of the play, we must surely take

Admetos' grief as sincere: there is more than a hint of real tragedy in his ἄρτι μανθάνω (940).

How, finally, does the last scene of the play affect our view of Admetos? It is interesting that Herakles gently but firmly expresses criticism of Admetos for concealing the truth: μέμφομαι μέν, μέμφομαι (1017). The suggestion seems to be that true friendship in fact lies in something more than a mechanical returning of χάρις for χάρις: it should involve a willingness to trust another person and to confide in them. But it is one of the numerous paradoxes of *Alkestis* that Herakles, in the very moment of blaming his φίλος for deceiving him, proceeds immediately to use deceit; and this brings us to the persuasion of Admetos by Herakles.

It has been said that Admetos' agreement to accept what he believes to be 'another woman' into his house is designed by Euripides to seem heavily ironical in view of his earlier promise (328 ff.) not to remarry. It is of course hard to disprove such a suggestion conclusively; but certain considerations tell against it. Firstly, the resistance of Admetos is extremely lengthy. At line 1020 Herakles instructs him to look after the woman, but only at line 1108 does Admetos consent to her entry into the house; and not until 1118— almost exactly a hundred lines since the original instruction was given—does he reluctantly agree to take her in himself. Given the compression and stylization of stichomythia—one may compare the handful of lines in which Klytaimnestra persuades Agamemnon in *Agamemnon*—Euripides can hardly be said to have portrayed Admetos acquiescing readily. Secondly, there is that much more pressure on Admetos to accept because to refuse would be to refuse a χάρις to a friend—and throughout the play we have seen and heard of several such favours which have been presented in a positive light, most notably Alkestis' χάρις of life to Admetos and Admetos' χάρις of hospitality to Herakles. Thirdly, does it not make a difference that, because of what the audience knows but Admetos does not, the audience *wants* him to acquiesce? The desired outcome, the outcome which will restore the relationship torn by Alkestis' self-sacrifice and Admetos' grief, the outcome which will enable Herakles worthily to reciprocate Admetos' gift of hospitality—that outcome depends on Admetos' giving way. Often enough in his other works Euripides uses irony to expose the reality behind human pretension; but there is no reason why we should deny him the right to be unironical if that was what the drama required.

5. *The tone of 'Alkestis': tragedy? comedy? 'fourth play'?*

Alkestis is unique amongst the surviving works of the Greek tragedians in that it is the only one of which we know both that it was put on fourth and that it was not a satyr-play. Scholars have tried to accommodate this uniqueness by inventing the term 'pro-satyric'; but this does little more than remind us that there is an unusual phenomenon which needs explanation.[37] However, the impulse to coin such a term is not wholly misguided, since it reflects the importance of our being able to reconstruct the category—the mental 'heading'—to which the original audience would have ascribed the play. After all, some sense of what the Athenians would have expected from *Alkestis* is necessary before we can judge how far Euripides met, or perhaps challenged, those expectations. But how do we proceed if we have no other work which we can be certain is a non-satyric fourth play?

Faute de mieux we may consider satyr-plays themselves. To answer the question, 'What would the audience have expected from a fifth-century satyr-play?', we have to rely mainly on Sophokles' *Ichneutai* and Euripides' *Kuklops*, the only two examples to have survived in anything like complete form. The subject of *Ichneutai* is the theft of the cattle of Apollo by baby Hermes; helping in the quest for the lost beasts are Silenos and his sons the Satyrs. In other words the plot is, like the plots of tragedy, taken from the mythical past, but bursting into it is a disruptive and indeed farcical element. *Kuklops* too is set in the mythical past, and includes many of the features from *Odyssey* ix: Polyphemos' cannibalism; Odysseus' trick with the name; the blinding; the escape. But into this traditional world of myth there bursts, as before, an element of disruptive farce: once again it is the lustful and cowardly Satyrs with their pot-bellied old father. Amongst many amusing moments perhaps the best is when Polyphemos, hopelessly drunk, ominously announces that he prefers boys to women, and carries off the alarmed Silenos into his cave to be his Ganymedes.

The rest of our evidence about satyr-plays,[38] meagre though it is, does not invalidate the assumption that the audience awaiting the start of such a work was expecting something set in the mythical past, but with a disruptively comical element breaking in to disturb the seriousness. But what about *non*-satyric fourth plays? While we really cannot be dogmatic about audience-expectations in this case, it is at any rate interesting that in *Alkestis* too we find a combination of a mythical setting with an element of disruptive comedy, as Herakles totters on to the stage after enjoying himself in Admetos' wine store.

Alkestis is indeed a quite remarkably variegated work. It has many features in common with tragedy: an οἶκος is disrupted; a character is caught in dilemmas (be hospitable, or mourn; accept the gift of life and live emptily, or die and render the gift meaningless); events come to a crisis; a father and son are driven to a bitter scene of mutual recrimination; someone learns the truth too late. On the other hand, Herakles' riotous good spirits, and the loving reconciliation at the end, may make us think rather of comedy. But it has to be said that the serious part of the play far exceeds the light-hearted. Could it be that Euripides was surprising his audience in 438 by providing something darker and more thought-provoking than they were expecting from a fourth play? We have no way of answering the question for certain. It is better simply to rejoice in the particular—indeed unique—range of emotions and tones which make up this rich and complex masterpiece.[39]

R. G. A. Buxton
University of Bristol

FOOTNOTES

[1] Apollo emerges from house: see N. C. Hourmouziades, *Production and imagination in Euripides* (Athens 1965) 162–3. Symbolism of Apollo leaving and Thanatos entering the house: J. Dingel, *Das Requisit in der griechischen Tragödie* (Diss. Tübingen 1967) 213, followed by A. Rivier, 'En marge d'*Alceste* et de quelques interprétations récentes', *MH* xxix (1972) 124–40, at 130. (There is virtually nothing on *Alk.* in E. H. Haight, *The symbolism of the house door in classical poetry* [New York 1950].)

[2] Schol. *Alk.* 98, 99; Aristoph. *Ekkl.* 1033; Pollux viii 65–6; *cf.* D. C. Kurtz and J. Boardman, *Greek burial customs* (London 1971) 146, and R. Parker, *Miasma* (Oxford 1983) 35.

[3] See W. Steidle, *Studien zum antiken Drama* (Munich 1968) 146, with n. 76.

[4] Hermes Thuraios: *cf.* L. R. Farnell, *The cults of the Greek states* (Oxford 1896–1909) v, 66 n. 23, and Eitrem in *RE* viii 777.

[5] Linguistic connections between words meaning 'door' and 'outside': see E. Benveniste, *Indo-european language and society* (Eng. trans. London 1973) 255–6.

[6] Groom holds bride χεῖρ' ἐπὶ καρπῷ: see Ian Jenkins, 'Is there life after marriage?', *BICS* xxx (1983) 137–45; the significance of the gesture in *Alk.* is noted by H. P. Foley, *Ritual irony* (Ithaca 1985) 87–8.

[7] Bride carried over threshold in Rome: refs. listed by M. B. Ogle, 'The house-door in Greek and Roman religion and folklore', *AJPh* xxxii (1911) 251–71, at 253.

[8] θυρωρός: Sappho *fr.* 110 LP; Pollux iii 42; Hesych. s.v.; see also Theoc. 15. 77 with Gow *ad loc.* We may add that the literary lover/suitor only got as far as the *house* door, which was where he sang his *paraklausithuron*; *cf.* F. O. Copley, *Exclusus amator*, Amer. Philol. Assoc. monograph 17 (1956).

[9] Welcome by groom's parents: schol. Eur. *Phoin.* 344 (mother); Sabouroff loutrophoros, illustration and refs. in Jenkins (n.6) = Daremberg/Saglio s.v. 'matrimonium', fig. 4866 (mother and father); Berlin cup, Beazley *ARV²* 831, 20 (mother); Louvre pyxis, Beazley *ARV²* 924, 33 = E. Pfuhl, *Malerei und Zeichnung der Griechen* (Munich 1923) pl. 580 with pp. 568–9 (? mother and father).

[10] Good remarks on this in A. P. Burnett, 'The virtues of Admetus', *CPh* lx (1965) 240–55, repr. in *Oxford readings in Greek tragedy*, ed. E. Segal (Oxford 1983) 254–71, esp. 269.

[11] On death as a process see now Robert Garland, *The Greek way of death* (London 1985) 13.

[12] See Dale's commentary on 871.

[13] Hom. *Il.* xxiv 93–4, *Od.* viii 92; *Hom. H. Dem.* 40 ff.; Plato *Phd.* 117c; etc.

[14] *Her. Main.* 1160–2, with Bond's commentary *ad loc.*

[15] Luc. *Symp.* 8: πάνυ ἀκριβῶς ἐγκεκαλυμμένη. An *onos* from Eretria (Beazley *ARV*² 1250–1, 34, Arias/Hirmer *HGVP* pl. 203) shows Alkestis veiled in the company of women—possibly before the wedding.

[16] John H. Oakley, 'The Anakalupteria', *Arch.Anz.* 1982, 113–18.

[17] L. Deubner, 'ΕΠΑΥΛΙΑ', *JDAI* xv (1900) 144–54.

[18] So rightly P. Roussel, 'La famille athénienne', *Lettres d'humanité* ix (1950) 5–59, at 10.

[19] For vases depicting wedding processions see C. H. E. Haspels, 'Deux fragments d'une coupe d'Euphronios', *BCH* liv (1930) 422–51; J. Boardman, 'Pottery from Eretria', *ABSA* xlvii (1952) 1–48, at 34–5; I. Krauskopf, 'Eine attisch schwarzfigurige Hydria in Heidelberg', *Arch.Anz.* 1977, 13–37. Examples of 'veiled' bride—i.e. bride with head covered—in bridal procession: Sabouroff loutrophoros, Berlin cup and Louvre pyxis as cited in n. 9 above; hydria from Orvieto (in Florence, Mus.Nat.) showing Peleus and Thetis on marriage chariot, Beazley *ABV* 260, 30; pelike in Louvre showing veiled bride being led χεῖρ' ἐπὶ καρπῷ, Beazley *ARV*² 250, 15.

[20] Pollux ii 59, iii 36; *cf.* Deubner (n. 17) 148.

[21] Eurydike too is veiled during her transition from death to life: see the fifth-century relief of Orpheus, Eurydike and Hermes (known from Roman copies, *cf.* H. A. Thompson, *Hesperia* xxi [1952] 60 ff., with pl. 17a, and E. B. Harrison, *Hesperia* xxxiii [1964] 76 ff., with pl. 12d).

[22] There are further links between the hood and 'death': the monk is surrounded, when prostrate, by 'catafalque' candles; and monks are buried with the hood *up*. (I am indebted for guidance here to Dr Ian Hamnett.)

[23] *Life* of Aischylos, 6 (= Aisch. *fr.* 243a M); see O. Taplin, 'Aeschylean silences and silences in Aeschylus', *HSCP* lxxvi (1972) 57–97, at 60–2.

[24] The 'third day' detail (*cf.* Aisch. *fr.* 212a M) is accepted for *Myrmidons* by Taplin (n. 23) 64. In *Phrygians* Achilles' motive for veiling seems to have been grief; in *Myrmidons* it may have been because of his self-imposed marginality; see Taplin, 76.

[25] Eur. *Hipp.* 275.

[26] *Eum.* 448 ff. For the converse see *Eum.* 276–7 and esp. 287: when Orestes' pollution has gone, he speaks ἀφ' ἁγνοῦ στόματος. N.b. also Eur. *I.T.* 951 and 956 for the silence surrounding the polluted Orestes at Athens.

[27] The revived dead: Plu. *Quaest.Rom.* 264f–265a, Hesych. s.v. δευτερόποτμος. See G. G. Betts, 'The silence of Alcestis', *Mnemosyne*, 4th series, xviii (1965) 181–2, and R. Parker (n. 2) 61.

[28] Pollux iii 36.

[29] A word needs to be added about Admetos' assertion (357 ff.) that, had he the voice of Orpheus, he would have gone down to charm the powers of the underworld. One implication is, of course, that Admetos does *not* have the voice of Orpheus; hence the outlook in Admetos' own case would seem (as with the references to Asklepios) to be made even more pessimistic. On the other hand, it is not clear what version of the Orpheus/Eurydike story had the greater currency in Euripides' time—did he look back and lose her, or was his mission successful? If the latter alternative were being evoked, the reference to Orpheus might offer a small glimmer of hope that the boundary between life and death *can* be affected by human entreaty.

[30] Justina Gregory appropriately describes Herakles in this play as 'the restorer of differences', 'Euripides' Alcestis', *Hermes* cvii (1979) 259–70, at 267.

[31] One may consult A. Brelich, *Gli eroi greci* (Rome 1958); G. K. Galinsky, *The Herakles theme* (Oxford 1972); and M. S. Silk, 'Herakles and Greek tragedy', *G&R* xxxii (1985) 1–22.

[32] *Cf.* Silk (n. 31) 7.

[33] Trans. slightly adapted from Gulick, Loeb edn.

[34] See Garland (n. 11) 41 on the varying relationship between pollution and degrees of kinship in Greece.

[35] An example is W. D. Smith, 'The ironic structure in *Alcestis*', *Phoenix* xiv (1960) 127–45, who sees the play's apparently positive verdict on Admetos undercut by 'a running commentary which hints at kinds of motivation and qualities of character beneath the surface' (134); on this reading Admetos emerges as 'self-centred, cowardly, and short-sighted' (129). For similarly unflattering views of Admetos see K. von Fritz, *Antike und moderne Tragödie* (Berlin 1962) 256–321, esp. 310; and E.-R. Schwinge, *Die Verwendung der Stichomythie in den Dramen des Euripides* (Heidelberg 1968) 109.

[36] *Art. cit.* (n. 10). Another non-ironist is that fine Euripidean A. Rivier; see *art. cit.* (n. 1), with sequel at *MH* xxx (1973) 130–43.

[37] Dana F. Sutton suggests other possible candidates for the category 'pro-satyric'; see *The Greek satyr play* (Meisenheim am Glan 1980) 184–90.

[38] Recently collected and analysed by Richard Seaford in the introduction to his edn of *Cyclops* (Oxford 1984).

[39] This is an expanded version of a paper given at the Hellenic Society Colloquium for Prof. Winnington-Ingram; my thanks are due to the audience for their constructive comments, and in particular to Ian Jenkins for subsequent assistance. The same material also formed the basis of a lecture given in Greek in the Department of Classical Philology at Ioannina; the ensuing discussion was of great value to me, particularly the contributions by Mary Mantziou, Katerina Synodinou, Andreas Katsouris and D. Sakalis. The present paper is substantially the same as that which appears in *Dodoni: Philologia* xiv (1985), 75–90, and is printed here with the kind permission of the editors of that journal.

Mothers' Day[1]

A note on Euripides' Bacchae

The illusion of critical progress, I have the feeling, is very largely sustained by the simple expedient of forgetting what our predecessors have written. To go back to Professor Winnington-Ingram's *Euripides and Dionysus* more than thirty years after first reading it, and, incredibly, almost fifty years after his first writing it, was an astonishing and chastening experience: he has said so much; so much that one might have wanted to say. So much, that all I can offer in this paper is a sort of extended footnote to his text, the suggestion of a slightly different point of view from which to read the play—a suggestion made in admiration rather than disagreement.[2]

Among the Yoruba-speaking peoples of Western Nigeria and Benin, there is a festival at the beginning of the spring rains called Efe/ Gelede. The festival is held to honour 'the mothers', sometimes called 'our mothers, the witches'; it is 'an occasion for publicly acknowledging the underlying power and authority, *ashe*, of women and the ambivalences that such a power creates in a patrilineal and patrilocal society. For it is not only the creative power of woman, manifest in the mystery of birth and the affective ties of nurturing, but fear of the secret and destructive powers known in witchcraft that shape Yoruba male self-understanding.'[3] The masks that are worn in the Gelede dances show a delicate, serene, 'cool' face surmounted by a towering bladed superstructure, like the 'feathers of an enormous bird . . . rising from the forehead'. The 'fixed stare' of the eyes conveys 'a gaze that begins to claw at the imagination', a gaze 'that devours with a benign indifference', 'an awesome, consuming power'. *Bacchae* has been described to me (by my wife, I should perhaps add) as Euripides' ultimate play about women. I think that description is illuminating, and it is a reading of *Bacchae* as a play about women and about mothers that I want to put forward in this paper.

'The Mothers' might indeed be an illuminating alternative title to the play. The arch of the play's structure is supported by two mothers, sisters, Semele and Agaue, victims and doers of violence, the one blasted to smouldering ash within the house in which she gave birth, the other tearing limb from limb on the green mountainside (χλωραῖς ὑπ' ἐλάταις) the son she had born and nurtured. It is as nursing mothers that we first see the women of Thebes in the forest of oak and pine on Kithairon: the first messenger describes them (699 ff.) nurturing their young with the milk of their breasts, but the nurture is displaced onto the young of wild animals (deer and wolves). When the mothers descend on the villages of Hysiae and Erythrae, children are first among the booty that they 'sieze' (754). In the opening lines of the play, Dionysus returns ('comes': ἥκω) to Thebes as 'son of Zeus', to the starkly presented, still smouldering ruins of the house where his mother, 'of the thunder-flash', was destroyed as she gave birth by the lightning of his father, the place of her death now an *abaton* (10) marked by the miraculous, luxuriant growth of Dionysus' vine (6–12). The association between birth, violent death and fertility is already established: it is the germ from which the play will grow. The mission of the son is to 'defend' his mother by the revelation of himself to men as *daimon* (φανέντα θνητοῖς δαίμονα) and as 'son of Zeus' (41 f.; cf. 22). As the play's end approaches, Pentheus is netted and in his turn 'comes' (ἥξει: 847) to the Bacchae on the mountain to pay his recompense, 'die at his mother's hands' and 'recognize the son of Zeus, Dionysus' ((847–61). It is his mother, 'priestess of bloodshed', who 'falls upon him' first, and as he calls her 'mother', not once but twice, and declares himself twice her son, as he 'strokes her cheek', she 'tears out' his arm from the shoulder (1114–28). The 'mother' takes his dismembered head in her arms and crowns with it her thyrsus (1139–42; cf. 966–9).[4] Other mothers also appear throughout the play. The Stranger describes the drums of the chorus as inventions not only of Dionysus but also of 'Mother Rhea' (58–9); in the parodos the chorus associate the mountain rituals of Dionysus with the *orgia* of Kybele, the 'great Mother' (78–9). The parodos goes on to develop the theme of birth; first, the god's double birth, as first his 'mother' gave him birth 'ejected' (ἔκβολον) from her womb amid the violence of 'flying thunder' and 'lightning stroke' (89–93), and then as Zeus bore him from the 'birth-chambers' of his thigh, a god 'horned, crowned with snakes' (94–103). The chorus move on without a break to call on Thebes, 'nurturer of Semele', to 'be luxuriant' (βρύετε) with ivy and bryony, with branches of oak and fir (the scene of birth is wrapped and bound in Dionysiac green and white), and from there to the birth-story of Zeus himself, and the drums and flutes of another mother, 'the Mother, Rhea' (128); on again to the dance on the mountains, to the 'joy', the 'benefaction' (*charis*) of eating flesh raw, and from that sudden violence immediately, in the following sentence, to miracles of creativity, milk and wine and honey ('nectar of bees') flowing over the earth (141–2), as the dance speeds on indifferently to mountains of Phrygia, of Lydia, where the 'wild one' (ὁ Βακχεύς) runs with the torch of Syrian cedar held high, flames and luxuriant hair (τρυφερὸν πλόκαμον: 150) streaming in the wind and drums beating. This is giddy stuff: the decisive precisions, the stiff, egocentric indicatives of the god's prologue speech have given way to a compulsive language of exclamations, imperatives and repeated words and phrases in which the chorus drifts and slides through a constantly shifting and blurring scene of passion, excitement and violence, always on the edge of hysteria. But in both prologue and parodos our sense of the *meaning* of this play comes from the constant juxtaposition of things that do not belong together and that require conflicting responses of the audience: violence in birth, green luxuriance in destruction, and both juxtapositions connect women and god, through a shared language.

In the larger frame of the play, this same ambivalence of association creates a deeper, more extensive unease, by connecting the very idea of growth and fertility in its widest sense with images of violence and destruction. When Agaue enters with her son's bloody head carried in her arms, she refers to what she holds as 'a tendril new cut (ἕλικα νεότομον) from the mountain' and as 'a bull-calf, its chin luxuriant with fresh growth beneath the crest of soft hair' (1169 f.; 1185–7). The luxuriance and softness of Pentheus' hair link him not only to Dionysus and the 'spreading hair' that pours down his cheeks, 'full of desire' (455–6, 493) and to the hair of the maenads entwined with snakes (102–4), but also to the green luxuriance of vegetation that everywhere in the play marks the 'dionysiac scene', both of forest-covered mountain and of Semele's Theban birth-giving tomb precinct. It is a scene given most concentrated expression in the images of the 'green pleasures of the glade' and the 'fronds of shadow-haired forest (σκιαροκόμοιο ... ἔρνεσιν ὕλας: 866–7, 875–6),[5] in which the fawn of the third stasimon escapes from the hunt.

The potentially subversive ambivalence of luxuriant hair has been well studied in Edmund Leach's classic article 'Magical Hair',[6] but the associations of luxuriant vegetation deserve further consideration. They are often classed as unambiguous signs of the *positive* aspect of divinity, testimony to the fertility which it is the (supposed) object of ritual to secure, but comparison with other instances of luxuriance may suggest another reading. The scenery of Odysseus' journey in the *Odyssey* more than once confronts him, and us as readers, with a setting of fertility and luxuriance, but one felt as ambivalent in its implications: the cypresses, alder and poplar, filled with nesting birds, and the vine, springs and luxuriant meadows of violets and celery that surround Calypso's cave with its burning hearth and scent of cedar and citron wood (*Od.* 5. 63–73); the wooded, goat-filled island, with its 'soft' water-meadows and poplars that lies across the water from the cave of Polyphemus (9. 116–41); the thicketed forest that encloses Circe's dressed stone palace and its uncanny tame-wild animals (10. 150, 210–19);[7] even the year-round luxuriance of Alkinoos' orchard, with its ever-ripening fruit trees and vines, is rendered ambiguous and un-natural by its symmetries, straight lines and geometric order (7. 112–32)—all these are settings of a richness and fertility that in each case is made by association ambiguous, eery and ultimately unreal. For the touchstone of the real in the *Odyssey* is offered us in 'rugged Ithaca', another island scene but this time palpably 'real': no meadows, no rich grazing land for horses, but a 'good nurturer' of men and goats (4. 600–08; 9. 27).[8] Luxuriant fertility in a Dionysiac context recurs in the miracles of the *Homeric Hymn*: here the miraculous sweet-smelling wine, the vine and ivy of *Hom. Hymn Dionysus* 35 ff. give way with terrifying suddenness to the lion and bear of 44 ff. Neither here nor in the *Odyssey* is luxuriance and fertility to be trusted, nor is it in *Bacchae*. The streaming hair, the curling tendrils and fronds of dionysiac fertility are not signs of the god's benignity but only seeming so.

So too with the women and the atmosphere of natural luxuriance and fertility that surrounds them. The scene of the first messenger's encounter with them is green, cool and shaded (684 ff.; cf. 38). It is dawn, and as the women wake to Agaue's cry (her *ololyge*) they loose their hair to fall to their shoulders, pull round them the animal skins and snakes that are now their dress as 'wild women' and give their breasts, the mothers among them, to fawns and wolfcubs, crowning themselves with ivy, oak and bryony. Their world, their appearance and their behaviour are marked by a magical fertility, but the miraculous springs of water out of rock, of wine and milk, and the honey that drips from their fennel rods are to be read as signs of the ambiguities latent in the creative power of women. Their acts are to the messenger 'strange' and 'awesome'; like the vine that suddenly hides Semele's still smoking tomb in Thebes itself, the women and their actions are incongruous and out of place: they have been 'stung' by Dionysus, removed from looms and shuttles (118–9), and like the miracles of the *Homeric Hymn*, these miracles are soon to be polluted by the blood of men and animals (765–7) and the quiet order that on first view marks the women for the messenger is precarious and hides another reality. Order and stillness are replaced in an instant by sudden flight and collective violence (680–716; 728 ff.)

Our sense of incompatibles coexisting in the world of *Bacchae* is underpinned by other aspects of language and of form. Examples of oxymoron in the play, above all in the language of the chorus, bring home, at times with an aggressive sharpness, the juxtaposition of incongruous perceptions: 'pleasure/grace/benefaction of eating raw' (ὠμοφάγον χάριν: 139); 'roofless rocks' (ἀνορόφοις ... πέτραις: the suggestion of openness and freedom, combined with the breaking down of barriers, is unmistakeable in ll. 37–8); the 'rainless streams' of the barbarian river that nonetheless 'fertilize' (ῥοαὶ καρπίζουσιν ἄνομβροι: 407–8); entrapping nets that are simultaneously 'close and dear' (φιλτάτοις ἐν ἕρκεσιν: 958). Metaphor and paradox cohere to shocking effect: Pentheus 'seated' as master upon the 'back' of the tree where he has been so gently placed by the god is yet held by it (ἔχουσα νώτοις δεσπότην ἐφήμενον: 1074), simultaneously safe, because beyond the 'energy' (προθυμία) of the women as they hurl their missiles, and trapped (ἀπορίᾳ λελημένος: 1101–2).

Pentheus poised between contradictions is one aspect of the language of *Bacchae*; the other is an almost untranslatable violence of metaphor (τεταύρωσαι; συγκεραυνοῦσαι; διεσφαίριζε: 922, 1103, 1136) which enacts a correspondingly increasing violence of behaviour. The 'stiffness' and 'severity' (the terms are Dodds') which critics have noted in the play do indeed set it apart from other works of Euripides' last decade: there are no actor arias, no duets, little astrophic lyric, slight use of *antilabe*. But we can exaggerate the difference and over-estimate the play's 'gravity' and 'order' (Dodds again), if we fail to respond adequately to such things as the play's use of extended stichomythia to construct whole scenes and the highly resolved trimeters of the dialogue. Both serve to create a formal tension and unease and a precarious, unpredictable movement of the verse that Euripides exploits elsewhere in his late work to sustain an ambiguous emotional atmosphere. Even in the play's opening moments the fluttering resolutions of Dionysus' prologue speech belie to our ear the cool, factual precisions of 'I am the son of Zeus, I come ... this is, this shall be ...' The syntax 'says' one thing (contrast the hesitancies and involutions of the prologue speeches of Electra in *Orestes* and Hermes in *Ion*), the metre something else, something at odds with coolness and control.

The ambiguities and antimonies of *Bacchae* have been exhaustively analysed by Charles Segal[9] as an exploration of 'the Dionysiac' in Greek culture. 'The spirit of contradiction ... is also the spirit of Dionysus'.[10] Of Dionysus and/or of women and mothers. The women and mothers of the play are possessed by Dionysus as the Thunderer (βρόμιος), the beat of their drums and their songs 'thunder' (ἐπιβρέμει, βαρυβρόμων: 151, 156); their god is the 'wild one' (βακχος, ὁ βάκχιος: n.b. πρόβακχος of their *daimon*, the Thunderer, 413), and they are 'wild women' (βάκχαι, βακχίδες). God and women exchange names and functions bewilderingly. But is the thunder and the wildness of the women that of the god, or his of them? Is this a play about divinity, or about women? The question is perhaps not to be asked, but it obtrudes itself in the wake of our response to the interweaving of god and women. In *Bacchae* Dionysus is feminized (ὁ θηλύμορφος ξένος, 353)[11]; Pentheus becomes a woman, in dress and behaviour, to go to meet his mother and the god (821 ff., 915 ff.). If, in the end, Dionysus is revealed as god, it is not in himself, as a power transfigured, but in the actions of women. The Stranger vanishes and a voice sounds, not 'of Dionysus', but 'Dionysus', as the messenger guesses (1078 f.): there follows stillness and silence, of plants and animals. There is a terrifying emptiness as the god vanishes and mother and son are left to come face to face, watched by the horrified messenger, and through his eyes by us: whatever else was hallucination in this play, this is not.

Emptiness, the absence of what should be present, is a recurring feature in the world of *Bacchae*. At the outset, the Thebes to which Dionysus returns is an empty city, its women displaced from their homes and proper occupations onto the green mountainside, its king 'outside' the country (32–8, 215), its streets empty for the god's procession (69 ff., 83 ff.); inside are old men and barbarian women from the holy mountains of Lydia. Above all an emptiness of the male. Sexual activity is everywhere implicit in the play, not just in the prurient fantasies of Pentheus, but as counterpart to the images of luxuriance and fertility, whereas sexually active males are strikingly absent. There are no adult males, no fathers, only the old and inadequate, and the young and inexperienced. Pentheus is ὁ νεανίας (274, 974, 1254: cf. 1185–7, and τέκνον 1308, 1317); Dionysus, ὁ δαίμων ὁ νέος (256, 272) who may do τι νέον (362), is not merely 'new' but also 'young', unbearded, adolescent, like his victim.

Dionysus is 'of Thebes', but also and simultaneously 'from elsewhere' (461 ff.): the motif of displacement and bilocation also associates women and god. The women are divided and polarised: the Theban women on the mountain, the mountain women of Lydia in the city. But like the god they too offer an image of belonging and not belonging, of being simultaneously in and out of place, that is uncanny. But it is of their essence. Women in *Bacchae* share with divinity double-sidedness, gentleness, quiet and release alternating with explosive violence. They also share as mothers the co-presence of fertility, nurture and destructiveness that marks the god, not the comfortable fertility of Teiresias' reductionist 'placing' of Dionysus within an intellectual schema as the liquid complement to Demeter's dry nourishment (274–85), but a fertility that is everywhere indissociable from violence, from images of fire, of tearing, blasting (n.b. συγκεραυνοῦσαι (1103) with its associations with Zeus himself) and blood.

What we see in *Bacchae* is a world emptied of men, in which the overriding strength, 'the force that through the green fuse drives the flower', is with women and with the female. It is a world in which creativity is allied to violence and the link is blood. Before the death of Pentheus the chorus foresee the scene on the mountain in which 'the mother', Agaue, is first to catch sight of the 'frenzied spy on the mad women' in his woman's dress: they imagine her shouting to the mad women: 'who is this, who . . . has come to the mountain, to the mountain? Who was his mother? He was not born from the blood of women, this one, he is the offspring of some lioness or of Libyan Gorgons' (980–90). They are wrong: Pentheus is born of woman, 'of the blood' of woman. When Agaue's vision clears, it reveals him to her no longer as a lion but as the son she bore in her house, the 'shoot' (ἔρνος) of her womb, in Kadmos' words of grief over the destruction of the house (1306): natural birth has ended in unnatural death. In their last, brief song before Agaue's entry the chorus sang of her 'glorious triumph—to lay her hand red in her son's blood' (1163–4). Fertility and violence are linked in blood. In *Bacchae* Euripides presents a world that recalls Geoffrey Hill's lines:

'By blood we live, the hot, the cold . . .
There is no bloodless myth will hold.'[1][2]

J. GOULD
University of Bristol

[1] The version of this paper read to the Hellenic Society's Colloquium for Professor Winnington-Ingram was given under the title 'The Return of the *Bacchae*'. As the following day was, in Britain, Mothering Sunday, I suggested 'Mothers' Day' as an alternative title: I have adopted it here because it indicates more clearly the drift of the argument I put forward in this essay, and also as a reminder that the day of the first performance of *Bacchae* was also the day of the first performance of *Iphigeneia at Aulis* and to draw attention to the dramatic importance of the mother's relationship with her child in that play too. I hope to discuss the implications of this juxtaposition of imaginary worlds on another occasion.

[2] A footnote also to my own essay 'Law, Custom and Myth: Aspects of the social position of women in classical Athens' (*J.H.S.* 100 [1980], 38–59). The anxiety attaching to mother/child relationships and to the 'meaning' to be given to the power of women in a man's world is as potent a source of creative tension in *Bacchae* as in any of the contexts I discuss in that essay.

[3] John Pemberton in W. Fagg, J. Pemberton 3rd and B. Holcombe (eds.), *Yoruba Sculpture of West Africa*, New York, 1982, 56; cf. also ibid. 62, 110, 150, 192.

[4] Georges Devereux, in his painstaking examination of the psychiatric implications of the Agaue scene (*J.H.S.* 90 [1970], 35–48) does not note the evident phallic symbolism of the son's head impaled on the mother's thyrsus: it may perhaps be seen as further indication of the 'sickness' of the mother/son relationship in *Bacchae*. As a key to Greek perceptions of Agaue's action, we may compare the passages cited by Dodds on *Bacchae* 1141: Hector's desire to impale the head of Patroclus in *Il.* 18. 176 f. and the Aeginetan Lampon's suggestion to Pausanias that he impale the head of Mardonius in revenge for Mardonius' similar desecration of Leonidas' head at Thermopylae (Her. 9. 78; 7 238). We may add Her. 4. 103 where impaling the head is part of the more horrific account of the barbarian Taurians' treatment of shipwrecked strangers. The Taurians act thus 'when aroused' (this is surely the meaning of ἐπανεχθέντες) and in all cases the act is seen as one of ultimate degradation, both of victim and agent.

[5] Compare the phrase λευκοτρίχων πλοκάμων used of the στέμματα that tie the bacchants' fawnsskins of the parodos: 112.

[6] E. Leach, 'Magical Hair', *Journal of the Royal Anthropological Institute*, 88 (1958), 147–64.

[7] See also *J.H.S.* 100 (1980), 52–3.

[8] Norman Austin's sensitive analysis of the relationship between landscape and 'character' in the *Odyssey* (*Archery at the Dark of the Moon*, California, 1975, 143–71) declines to use the Ithacan landscape as a 'control' on the implications of fertility elsewhere in the poem, preferring to see Ithaca rather as a paradigm of social disorder. But the dung-heap in the courtyard (*Od.* 17. 296 ff.; Austin, op. cit., 169–70) is as much a mark of the 'reality' of the Ithacan scene as of its disordered society.

[9] C. Segal, *Dionysiac Poetics and Euripides' Bacchae*, Princeton, 1982.

[10] Segal, op. cit., 8.

[11] Not only, of course, in *Bacchae*: cf. Aeschylus, fr. 61 Radt; the Aeschylean question—'where is the woman from?—significantly associates Dionysus' femininity with his being from elsewhere.

[12] Geoffrey Hill, 'Genesis', in *For the Unfallen*, Andre Deutsch, 1959.

Some problems of a translator

Ours might be termed an age of translation. Never have the ancient classics been more available to the ordinary reader. If one wishes to read the *Odyssey* in translation one may choose from several up-to-date translations from Rieu & Lattimore to Fitzgerald & Shewring. For the *Oresteia* there are even more—Thomson, Vellacott, Lattimore, Fagles, Lloyd-Jones and most recently Harrison. For the *Trojan Women*, which I am currently translating, there is a range from Vellacott and Lattimore and Curry to radical adaptions like Sartre's version later translated into English by Ronald Duncan. The spectrum of available translations is wide, going from prose or verse (with varying degrees of closeness to the text) to the more radical 'creative adaptations' like Christopher Logue's *Patroclea* or Annouilh's *Antigone*.

Now obviously this range and availability of translation is in one way a very good thing—and has done much for our subject. It spells confidence in the values of past literature and a commendable wish to communicate those values. But I wonder whether this confidence does not at times topple into an overconfidence which has its dangers.

Students from other disciplines than classics, and with no Greek, are all too often inclined these days to assume that a good translation *is* the original and that they can confidently pronounce upon its finer nuances from the translation. This is particularly dangerous where high poetic language is involved. I remember one student building a whole essay on the subject of image patterns from what she took to be an original image in the *Trojan Women*, that of 'the lonely seagull'. It has no counterpart in the original but was a translator's image which set up a completely different set of resonances from the original words. I remember another student who because of the ambiguity of the English word 'love' and a misunderstanding of the difference between φιλία and ἔρως in Greek built a false theory about concepts of love in the *Antigone*.

Although it is an excellent thing from most points of view that a student can find the ancient poets readable and accessible in his own language, and although it is splendid that people continue to feel they can translate an ancient text into modern idiom, I want this afternoon to introduce a note of caution and to give two examples of what I regard as extreme limitations for the translator, and consequently, for his interpreters.

The two kinds of problem I propose to discuss are (a) the shifting values in different categories of vocabulary at different times and the problems this poses for the translator, and (b) the difficulty the translator has in conveying lyric language and particularly the gap between traditional resonances and new contexts which the language of tragic lyric brings with it.

The minimum aim of the translator must be to achieve 'translucency' to use Eliot's word, but even with this minimum aim the translator finds that he is trapped by his own age in ways of which he may not be fully aware. He may discover that the weight of words available to him which lie behind habits of emotion and thought characteristic of our own century are driving him into paths which somehow distort the original. However faithful he may try to be to his source, changes of phrasing, feeling, tone, nuance, ornament and form—some merely due to the different structure or vocabulary of the languages involved—but not all—will creep in despite his best endeavours.

Here is an example of the havoc the changing weight of words may produce, my category (a).

The *Trojan Women* is a play about acute suffering—about pain, damage, loss and violence, and in attempting to translate it the translator has particular difficulties in addition to the usual ones associated with rendering Greek Tragedy. For so much of this play is prolonged lament for that suffering and the expression of concentrated grief. The Greek conveys a rich range of words expressing the emotions of grief. Yet when we examine our own vocabulary we are hampered at every turn in trying to find modern equivalents. Consider for instance some of their many verbs describing the utterance and feeling of lament: θρηνέω, θρηνωδέω, αἰάζω, ἐξαιάζω, θροέω, στενάζω, καταστένω, ἰαχέω, θωύσσω, κωκύω, ὀλοφύρομαι, ἀπολοφύρομαι, οἰμώζω, κατοιμώζω, ἐξοιμώζω, γοάομαι, δακρύω, κλαίω

If one looks these up in the dictionary one finds that the same English words are given again and again to translate them.

e.g.   θρηνέω: wail, bewail
         αἰάζω, ἐξαιάω: bewail, bemoan
         ὀλοφύρομαι: bewail, lament, mourn

ἰαχέω, ἰάχω: cry, shriek in pain
στενάζω: bewail, bemoan, groan

and so on.

It is partly that we lack the range in English to cope with these words and partly because where we *do* find equivalents they sound outdated and lacking in weight. 'Lament, bewail, bemoan' do not have a contemporary ring. And many words which in Victorian times did justice to the emotion of grief—particularly abstract nouns, now sound oldfashioned. Notice that I chose factual words just now to describe the play's action. 'Pain', 'damage', 'loss' and 'violence' still have some impact. But consider others more emotional, now outworn. What a hollow ring they have: 'affliction, anguish, woe, sorrow' and even 'care, distress, grief and agony'. Our vocabulary has grown tired and only a few words in this area still carry their full weight. 'Pain' is one. 'Hurt' is another. But those words have factual as well as emotional connotations. It is the words for *feelings* which have shrunk. Take also the Greek apostrophes αἰαῖ, αἰαῖ; φεῦ, φεῦ; ἒ, ἔ; οἴμοι; ἰώ, ἰώ, ὀτοτοῖ which in that language express so adequately raw feelings. 'Alas', 'alack', 'woe' is me' sound ludicrous. And how is one to differentiate between them? I admit defeat here. Sometimes one can give a periphrasis like 'How wretched I feel', but at other times in my translation I have kept the Greek sounds transliterated. There simply are no modern substitutes that I know of.

Take another area—that of religious feeling. Part of the point of this play is that the characters feel that even the Gods have deserted them. 'The gods loved Troy once. Now they have forgotten'. (857–8) The power of that sense of loss resides in the assumption that the Trojans *believed* in their gods, performed their sacrifices, were devout, but in spite of this were let down by them. This is the point of the rich description of Troy's altars burning with incense and sacrifices, and the images in the third stasimon. Zeus betrayed all this devotion, οὕτω δὴ . . . προύδωκας (1060–2) the ode begins. It is very difficult for a modern audience to capture the impact of this betrayal when deep religious feeling today is on the whole rare. Once again words for religious experience in English sound tired and outmoded 'reverence, veneration, devotion, devoutness, sanctity, sacredness, piety, holiness, godly, blessed, pious, holy'. It was because the Greeks had such a strong sense of the gods and the supernatural at work that they used words like δυσδαίμων, βαρυδαίμων, δύσμορος, δυστύχης. Yet English equivalents like 'hapless', 'ill-starred', 'ill-fated' sound quaint today and purely secular words like 'miserable' and 'wretched' do not get that sense of the supernatural.

This poverty of words available to express religious feeling and the poverty of the concepts behind the words is particularly evident in a context like Cassandra's aria where there is a great concentration of Greek words for religious observance, and for the ceremony of marriage within a religious context, e.g. ἱερόν (309), σέβω (308), ὅσιος (329), θυηπολῶ (330), the five times repeated refrains to the Marriage God, Ω 'Ὑμέναι' ἄναξ, the address to Hecate and Apollo, and the Bacchic cry εὐᾶν, εὐοῖ as well as words with religious connotations like μακάριος four times repeated and stressed through being at the beginning of lines (3 times) and once a superlative at the end. The ode is saturated with the vocabulary of worship and the effect of this aria depends upon the frenzied religious fervour of this priestess which has become distorted through madness. To make this song live for a modern audience with the same obsessive power that it presumably once had is extremely difficult.

I asked my students the other day which area they thought in our own language *did* still carry richness of emotional association where words still carried some force, and they said those of fear and horror. 'Fear: fright: terror: panic, alarm, shock, scare: consternation: dismay, qualms, misgivings, apprehension: unease: worry, nerves: jitters. Being petrified, terrified, panic-struck, flabbergasted, stunned, appalled, numbed, paralysed,' and so on. These words they said had not lost their impact.

I suspect also that physical words expressing *violence* of various kinds have not lost their force and that for us therefore, interestingly, there may be fewer problems in conveying the impact of a messenger speech than, say, a lyric lament.

It is with such shifting values of words that the translator has to contend, in addition to all the other difficulties with which the conventional language of Greek Tragedy presents him. For it did not of course resemble ordinary colloquial conversation.

It was a highly artificial poetic vocabulary and style removed from everyday naturalism, and yet at the same time it was a language which lived, and whose resonances were full of familiarity with earlier poetical forms. A prose translation has to contend not only with loss of metre, verse form, and poetic style, but also with these resonances in a medium where the language is many-layered and uneven in style. There is the utmost distinction between the lyric and the iambic portions. This can be rendered in verse by different metre, but in prose is more difficult to mark.

In the lyrics of tragedy we find the most concentrated and exposed poetic forms. Here are elaborate descriptive epithets, metaphors, new coinages, elevated periphrases, new uses of vocabulary and resonances from earlier poetic forms. And it is here that the translator finds a lot of problems. I want to look at one or two which arise in the first stasimon of the *Trojan Women*, and will comprise my category (*b*).

Χο. ἀμφί μοι Ἴλιον, ὦ   [στρ.
    Μοῦσα, καινῶν ὕμνων
    ἆισον σὺν δακρύοις ὠιδὰν ἐπικήδειον·
    νῦν γὰρ μέλος ἐς Τροίαν ἰαχήσω,   515
    τετραβάμονος ὡς ὑπ' ἀπήνας
    Ἀργείων ὀλόμαν τάλαινα δοριάλωτος,
    ὅτ' ἔλιπον ἵππον οὐράνια
    βρέμοντα χρυσεοφάλαρον ἔνο-   520
       πλον ἐν πύλαις Ἀχαιοί·
    ἀνὰ δ' ἐβόασεν λεὼς
    Τρωϊάδος ἀπὸ πέτρας σταθείς·
    Ἴτ', ὦ πεπαυμένοι πόνων,
    τόδ' ἱερὸν ἀνάγετε ξόανον   525

    Ἰλιάδι Διογενεῖ κόραι.
    τίς οὐκ ἔβα νεανίδων,
    τίς οὐ γεραιὸς ἐκ δόμων;
    κεχαρμένοι δ' ἀοιδαῖς
    δόλιον ἔσχον ἄταν.   530

    πᾶσα δὲ γέννα Φρυγῶν   [ἀντ.
    πρὸς πύλας ὡρμάθη,
    πεύκαν οὐρεῖαν, ξεστὸν λόχον Ἀργείων,
    καὶ Δαρδανίας ἄταν θεᾶι δώσων,   535
    χάριν ἄζυγος ἀμβροτοπώλου·
    κλωστοῦ δ' ἀμφιβόλοις λίνοιο ναὸς ὡσεὶ
    σκάφος κελαινὸν εἰς ἕδρανα
    λάϊνα δάπεδά τε, φονέα πατρί-   540
       δι, Παλλάδος θέσαν θεᾶς.
    ἐπὶ δὲ πόνωι καὶ χαρᾶι
    νύχιον ἐπεὶ κνέφας παρῆν,
    Λίβυς τε λωτὸς ἐκτύπει
    Φρύγιά τε μέλεα, παρθένοι δ'   545
    ἄειρον ἅμα κρότον ποδῶν
    βοάν τ' ἔμελπον εὔφρον', ἐν
    δόμοις δὲ παμφαὲς σέλας
    πυρὸς μέλαιναν αἴγλαν

    † ἔδωκεν ὕπνωι †.   550

ἐγὼ δὲ τὰν ὀρεστέραν   [ἐπωιδ.
τότ᾽ ἀμφὶ μέλαθρα παρθένον
Διὸς κόραν ἐμελπόμαν
χοροῖσι· φοινία δ᾽ ἀνὰ   555
πτόλιν βοὰ κατέσχε Περ-
γάμων ἕδρας· βρέφη δὲ φίλι-
α περὶ πέπλους ἔβαλλε μα-
τρὶ χεῖρας ἐπτοημένας.
λόχου δ᾽ ἐξέβαιν᾽ Ἄρης,   560
κόρας ἔργα Παλλάδος.
σφαγαὶ δ᾽ ἀμφιβώμιοι
Φρυγῶν ἔν τε δεμνίοις
καράτομος ἐρημία
νεανίδων στέφανον ἔφερεν   565
Ἑλλάδι κουροτρόφον,
Φρυγῶν δὲ πατρίδι πένθος.

Chorus   Sing, Muse, of Ilium: sing with tears a song of death in new strain. For I shall sing an ode for Troy, how I, an unhappy captive, perished because of the four wheeled horse when the Achaeans left it at the gates, rattling to high heaven with its arms and magnificently decked out in gold trappings.

The people stood on the Trojan rock and shouted aloud 'Our troubles are over, go down and bring in the image sacred to the Trojan goddess, Zeus' daughter'. What young girl then, what old person, did not run from their houses? Happy in their songs they took to their hearts destruction in disguise.

The whole race of Trojans rushed to the gates to give the goddess the mountain pinewood, polished ambush of the Argives which was to be the destruction of Troy. It was a gift to the virgin goddess of the immortal steeds.

They brought it like the dark hull of a ship, with encircling ropes of spun flax, to the stone floor of the temple of the goddess Pallas. It was death to our country. And when the darkness of night came upon their exertion and their exhilaration, the Libyan pipe sounded and Phrygian strains, and young girls lifted pulsing feet as they sang light-hearted songs. Inside the houses the shining brightness of torch flares gave a dark flickering gleam amid sleep.

I for my part at that time was singing and dancing in the palace in honour of the mountain-dwelling daughter of Zeus.

A bloody shout went through the city and possessed the site of Troy. Beloved children clutched their mothers' dress with trembling hands. War was stalking from his hiding place. This was the work of Pallas. And at the altars there was the murder of Trojans and on the beds headless desolation yielded a prize of young women who would bear sons for Greece and bring pain to the homeland of Troy.

This stasimon, as the others in this play, concerns Troy and its people. The style is not philosophical or moral in tone but descriptive, and its imagery brings alive in sensuously evocative language the city's life on the night Troy was betrayed by the invasion through its gates of the Wooden Horse. Scenes of false jubilation are contrasted with the subsequent desolation when the Greeks rampaged through the private apartments of the palace. Every Trojan woman has lived through this experience and the telling of it is therefore at the heart of the play.

Its reality is built up by the dramatist in a series of images suggesting sight, sound and texture. Sight for instance in the magnificently gold decked horse, encapsulated in the single and unique compound χρυσεοφάλαρον; in the dark and sinister ship's hull used to compare the shape and colour of the horse; in the bright torch flares glowing in the dark expressed in the oxymoron μέλαιναν αἴγλαν and in the shaking hands of children, χεῖρας ἐπτοημένας clutching at their mothers' dress. Sound is evoked in the description of pipe calls (544), thudding feet (546), as well as in the bold image at 555–6 'a bloody shout possessed the city'. Texture is stressed in a number of epithets suggesting the material composition of things—'the mountain pinewood' (532) the 'polished ambush' (532), 'the circling ropes of spun flax' (537), and the stone temple floor (540). But it is not enough to separate out the effects on the senses, for they interpenetrate one another. Thus the sound of thudding feet and singing cuts through the darkness with its intermittent gleams of torchlight, so that sound and dark and light become indistinguishable. Thus a shout is described with a word which also has connotations of the redness of blood, φοινία (555) and an abstract word 'ambush' (533) is given a tangible, textural adjective to suggest the surface of wood within which it is hidden.

And as if purely descriptive language falls short—at the end the poet goes into metaphor. The Greeks' brutal decapitation of the Trojan men in their beds is evoked in two words καράτομος ἐρημία 'headless desolation', while the Trojan women, taken as so much human loot to breed sons to Greek men, are called a νεανίδων στέφανον ... κουροτροφόν a phrase so condensed that it is almost untranslatable in English except by using more words 'a crowning prize of young women fit to breed sons for Greece'.

One of the features of lyric is the descriptive compound epithet and you will see that there are eleven here, several of them clustered in the description of the Wooden Horse which dominates strophe, anti-strophe and epode. Four in the space of four lines at 516–20, two in two lines at 535–6, and three at the end in four lines 562–6. Of these eleven, nine are either new coinages by Euripides or used in a different sense here by him from usages in other authors. Three, χρυσεο-φάλαρος, ἀμβροτόπωλος, ἀμφιβώμιος are hapaxes, two only occur in Euripides and not before, i.e. ἐπικήδειος (only here and in the *Alexandros*), and τετραβάμων, and four appear in different senses from usual, i.e. ἀμφίβολος, καράτομος, ἔνοπλος and κουροτρόφος.

The translator's problem is (1) how to get across a compound epithet at all in English since the form is not natural to our language, (2) how to get the feeling of newness if it is a new coinage, (3) how to register the resonance from earlier poetry if that exists.

Take (1). χρυσεοφάλαρος and ἀμβροτόπωλος are six and five-polysyllabled words. Even if one makes up a compound in English like 'gold-bedecked' it does not get this sense of weight and length. And if one resorts to a periphrasis one misses the concentration of the single word. Moreover 'gold-bedecked', though a compound of sorts in English, misses the precision of meaning in the Greek, for what the word indicates is 'gold cheek pieces on the head harness of the horse'. And I challenge any translator to find an English compound which encompasses all that. Lattimore gets some of this sense when he translates the word by 'thin gold at its brows', but this is to sacrifice the compoundness and the single concentration of the one striking word. ἀμβροτόπωλος, an epithet apparently applied to Pallas, appears to mean 'of the immortal steeds' or 'Owner of the immortal horses'. Again it is almost impossible to get the striking effect of the single word in Greek. For one wonders whether the epithet is not highlight-ing here the appropriateness of the treacherous gift of a horse to the treacherous goddess who is associated with horses. But it is of course not only the compoundness of these hapaxes contained within the single word with which the translator must contend, but also the feeling of newness which they must have originally conveyed (2). Here too he may have to admit defeat.

There are further complications. Because of the difficulties in English with such forms it becomes impossible in a translation to register where the rich density of style created by these epithets occurs, and where it does not—and that perhaps might be significant.

In other words the stylistic pace of the original is not measured in a translation. Here for example the pace lingers over the depositing of the horse with a visual image to mark it, and then quickens as the people of Troy shout and stream out from their houses. There there are no elaborate epithets. The pace slows again with another visual picture of the slow dragging in of the horse, like a ship, into the temple—again marked by compounds—and speeds up again to describe the singing and dancing in false celebration—in much simpler language. Thus the Greek has a variety of pace not always reproducible in English.

To come now to (3)—the registering of resonances from earlier poetry—particularly Homer and Pindar. Here too the compound epithet plays its part along with the other elements such as metre, form, and phraseology which all work to create a climate of Homeric and also Pindaric echoes, against which the poet can build his new context.

I will take metre and form first and then come back to the compounds. Metrically this is a fairly simple ode mainly lyric iambics with strophe, antistrophe and epode. But one thing is startling about it—its dactylic beginning

$$- \cup \cup - \cup \cup -$$
$$- \cup - \quad - - -$$
$$- \cup \cup - \cup \cup - - - \cup \cup - - -$$

'Sing, Muse, of Ilium: sing with tears a song of death in new strain'. The metre and the appeal to the Muse here recalls the beginnings of the Iliad and Odyssey and the whole phrase ἀμφί μοι . . . ὦ Μοῦσα is the classic beginning of several Homeric hymns, e.g. those to Pan, Poseidon and Dionysus. Why should the poet wish to echo those features here? Not only because the theme of war is an epic one, as Lee says, but because an epic beginning signals something important, grand and impressive and the chorus wish to register some familiar credentials for this. But they then go on to imply in their subsequent words καινῶν ὕμνων that the old forms are due to be told in a new way and the Muse pressed into service for a new kind of song. A hymnos is usually a song of praise of gods and heroes but is here used as a song sung in sympathy for the victims of war. Moreover this is a lyric lament for Troy's destruction seen uniquely not through the eyes of warriors but through those of a group of women—the victims. The chorus' account is not the traditionally heroic one of glorifying war yet it deserves, the poet implies, to be as important as epic in what new things it has to observe. There is of course irony too in this measuring of old attitudes against new ones.

Such an arresting contrast between epic style and values, and present ones conveyed through metre and choice of words, should be reflected in a translation. Lattimore misses this. Vellacott's better gets the flavour.

> 'Come, Muse, in tears begin
> And sing strange dirges over Ilium's grave'.

Curry's rendering

> A song
> A new song
> We would sing . . .

gets nothing at all of the impressive opening—of the mention of Troy or of the Muse—and is very free.

The Homeric resonances are kept up through the ode in certain formal grammatical elements in the tmesis at 522, the epic genitive λίνοιο at 537—in the unaugmented epic form ἄειρον at 546 and also in the use of certain simple epithets favoured by Homer—ξεστόν 533, κελαινόν 538 and μέλαιναν 549. There is no way a translator can render special word endings or unaugmented forms and thus in missing the many tiny signs of a previous tradition he is losing a whole dimension available to an ancient audience who knew its poetry, but lost to us.

This dimension involves the registering of the gap between old epic and lyric tones and new contexts, a gap which the opening of the ode sets up. For the old adjectives here acquire new and sinister connotations where in previous poetry they were either neutral or glorious. It is not an ordinary object that is ξεστόν but a treacherous ambush. The 'black gleam'—an oxymoron unknown to Homer—is likewise ominous.

And here we come back to the compound epithets. These too suggest by their Pindaric and Homeric resonances a chasm between old and new contexts. Χρυσεοφάλαρος is an hapax legomenon but coined on the analogy of the many χρυσο- compounds in Pindar. There they are all decorative and complimentary, part of the rich golden world of Pindar. Here the horse, however, described as decked out in golden trappings is no noble creature but an artificial device whose false allurement leads the Trojans to their destruction. So the traditional word is used ironically in this new context of treachery and death. Κουροτρόφος in 566 is likewise given a new and sinister context. Used in Homer to describe the distinctive benign and nurturing qualities of Ithaca (Od. IX 27)

> Τρηχεῖ' ἀλλ' ἀγαθὴ κουροτρόφος
> My land is rugged but knows how to breed brave sons.

it is here used in a grisly metaphor involving the production of children as a result of rape. 'Head-severing desolation produced a crown of young women to breed sons to Greece and cause pain to the homeland of the Trojans'. A benign Homeric epithet has become something malignant.

Now all this fits in with the constant play in the ode between old and new communicated in so many different ways through metre, phraseology, grammatical form, and calculated use of earlier poetic vocabulary. How is a translator to render this? He cannot hope to catch all the cross rhythms and echoes which the Greek text alone can yield. And he can only mourn that so much pleasure is lost to the modern Greekless reader.

It is thus in lyric that the metre and formal poetic devices are at their most concentrated and dominant. But of course all through a play even a translator who uses verse is faced with metrical and stylistic devices he cannot reproduce. An example would be the change from distichomythia to stichomythia at *Troades* 69, or the change from iambics to trochaic tetrameter at *Troades* 444, or the change from short iambic and dactylic rhythm to hexameters at *Troades* 595, or the unreproducible combination of sound and syntactical structures which build up in Andromache's speech at *Troades* 740 ff. These are devices unique to Greek which control the pace, tone and mood of the original and do not transport easily.

And so it is that the translator faces formidable problems in many areas. I have tried to outline two of these areas, first that of his own vocabulary where the values and relative weights of words are always shifting so that the medium in which he works is often deficient and certainly never constant, and second the area of Greek lyric where he must confront many poetic devices which are alien to the structure and form of English and which may carry resonances often inaccessible now to us. The translator must always fail in some ways, and the reader of a translation is doomed never to possess the precision of language and sharpness of imagination which the original would give him, but what I think must be said in conclusion is that the miracle seems to be that in spite of these losses and limitations for both translator and reader, the sheer power of the original still shines through most translations of Greek tragedy (even the most pedestrian) and that the exercise of translating and of reading translations is still rewarding for both parties. After all if people—for instance non-classical students and scholars, particularly of the humane disciplines, amateur dramatic societies, professional theatrical producers, school teachers and pupils—can think the *Trojan Women* is a great play from a translation, when many of its refinements and subtleties are still unrevealed, then perhaps this tells us that the original must be very great indeed and deserves therefore to draw to it all the varied talents and skills of which our generation is capable, but should offer with a certain degree of humility.

SHIRLEY A. BARLOW
Eliot College, University of Kent at Canterbury

Notes on tragedy and epic

The relations between tragedy and epic are far too complex and elusive to be discussed in a short paper; what follows may best be described as preliminary notes, an attempt to sketch out one or two possible directions that a fuller discussion might take.

My starting point is Jean-Pierre Vernant's influential essay 'Le moment tragique',[1] in which Greek tragedy is seen as embodying the tensions between the past, as represented by heroic myth, and the present, as expressed in the life of the contemporary polis. This idea of tension is a more helpful one, I think, than that of some sort of cover or disguise: it makes better sense to think of the stories of Homer and the cyclic poets as a medium for the tragedians' self-expression than as something that can as it were, be 'taken off', to reveal the fifth-century reality underneath. Metaphors of this kind might imply that what the texts were saying to their contemporary audiences was something essentially independent of the imaginary world in which the stories were set. But this imaginary world or 'region of the mind' (to borrow a phrase of Arthur Miller's) is highly interesting and individual. It is a world of dignity and glamour, evoking an elegant, ceremonious society in which people speak and behave with elaborate courtesy, but it is not by any means a carbon copy of the world of the Homeric poems, any more than the idiom of tragic discourse which gives it expression is epic pastiche. All the time it makes links between past and present, through the heroes, who have a continuing power and presence in cult, through references to institutions of the audiences's own time which are traced back to the time in which the stories are set, and through an idiom which juxtaposes Homeric words and images with modern coinages and modes of argument. Within any particular play the mixture of old and new will vary in different passages, but overall what is striking and significant is the inter-penetration of these elements.

The implications are far-reaching. One of the most important is the suggestion that civilization goes back a long way. The elegance and dignity characteristic of tragedy are not—it is implied—a recent invention; they have their roots in the distant past. The poetry of the polis can thus appropriate the epic for its own purposes, suggesting that the character and institutions of the city, of Athens in particular, have a heroic ancestry and the validity of long-established tradition. So the dramatists could often combine a strong affirmation of (ideal) civic values with a thoroughly tragic illumination of the irresolvable tensions and difficulties of life in civilized society: we need think only of the *Supplices* of both Aeschylus and Euripides, or of *Eumenides*, *O.C.* or *Medea*. If one function of tragedy was to explore in dramatic form the problems of the polis, another was surely to celebrate its capacity, however precarious, to face and try to understand them.[2]

Another implication of the continuity between past and present is that our own historical perspective may be misleading. Familiar as we are with Adkins's contrast between self-assertive heroic values and the so-called 'quiet' or 'co-operative' virtues that came to be respected in the fifth century, we are tempted to see a play like *Ajax* as a study in the passing of an era. Ajax in Bernard Knox's terms is 'the last of the heroes';[3] Charles Segal calls him 'an anomaly, a remote, gigantic figure': Ajax typifies the values of a past which is (tragically) found to be obsolete, and he and his world must now be replaced by the values of Odysseus, 'the man skilled in those forensic, civic arts which Ajax rejects'.[4] But it is hard to reconcile this approach with the evident importance of the cult of Ajax at Salamis, which is certainly prefigured in the play through the intense debate over what is to happen to his corpse. The final preparations for the burial of Ajax with full honours seem to point to a future significance, and Peter Burian has shown how even at an earlier stage in the action the corpse is seen as a source of protection for suppliants: 'The body becomes in effect a hallowed place, for it is recognized to have the power of a hero's tomb even before the question of his burial is settled.'[5] Moreover, Ajax, not Odysseus, is at the emotional centre of the play, and it is his experiences—his madness and return to sanity, his suffering and shame, his endurance and future reputation—that concern us. Finally, one of the interesting subtleties of Sophocles' design is the way in which Ajax and Odysseus use the same language to talk about such things as change, and friends and enemies, themes of fundamental importance for our understanding of the play. One is left wondering how far the 'historical' perspective is really relevant to the understanding of *Ajax*.

We should also bear in mind a different sort of caveat. In much modern criticism of Greek tragedy there is a tendency to see the epic elements as functioning mainly by means of inversion, pointing the contrast between the heroic exemplar and the problematic present. No doubt they do sometimes work like this, but things are not always so simple. The interpenetration of language is so pervasive that we ought surely to look for a more complicated model.[6]

The use of animal imagery in tragedy is a good illustration of the dangers of too reductive an approach. Much has been written recently on the category of 'the wild' in tragedy, which has an obvious importance as the opposite of civilized human order. As Segal puts it, 'civilized life for the fifth century is unthinkable without the polis, a bounded space dividing the human world from the wild', and 'man is threatened by the beast world pushing up from below, but he is also illuminated by the radiance of the Olympian gods above'.[7] This kind of structuralist analysis in terms of the god/man/ beast axis is a broadly helpful one for the study of Greek tragedy, and no one would want to deny that beast imagery is often used by the tragedians to express the idea of a threat to the norms of the social order.[8] We need look no further than the eagles devouring the hare, the lion cub, the two-footed lioness and the wolf of the *Agamemnon* or the ambiguous snakes of the *Choephoroe*; but we must always be alert to the possibility that such language may have other functions which do not fit so easily into this scheme. After all, many of the images of 'the wild' that we meet in tragedy come from the world of nature not direct but *via* epic poetry, and this must have some effect on the way they function. A couple of examples will illustrate the kinds of issues that arise.

The Parodos of the *Agamemnon* opens with a famous simile:

δέκατον μὲν ἔτος τόδ᾽ ἐπεὶ Πριάμῳ
μέγας ἀντίδικος,
Μενέλαος ἄναξ ἠδ᾽ Ἀγαμέμνων,
διθρόνου Διόθεν καὶ δισκήπτρου
τιμῆς ὀχυρὸν ζεῦγος Ἀτρειδᾶν,
στόλον Ἀργείων χιλιοναύταν
τῆσδ᾽ ἀπὸ χώρας
ἦραν, στρατιῶτιν ἀρωγάν,
μέγαν ἐκ θυμοῦ κλάζοντες Ἄρη
τρόπον αἰγυπιῶν,
οἴτ᾽ ἐκπατίοις ἄλγεσι παίδων
ὕπατοι λεχέων στροφοδινοῦνται
πτερύγων ἐρετμοῖσιν ἐρεσσόμενοι,
δεμνιοτήρη
πόνον ὀρταλίχων ὀλέσαντες·

ὕπατος δ' ἀίων ἤ τις Ἀπόλλων
ἤ Πὰν ἤ Ζεὺς οἰωνόθροον
γόον ὀξυβόαν τῶνδε μετοίκων
ὑστερόποινον
πέμπει παραβᾶσιν Ἐρινύν.
οὕτω δ' Ἀτρέως παῖδας ὁ κρείσσων
ἐπ' Ἀλεξάνδρῳ πέμπει ξένιος
Ζεὺς πολυάνορος ἀμφὶ γυναικός.

40–62

It is now the tenth year since Priam's
great adversary at law,
King Menelaus and Agamemnon,
the pair of sons of Atreus mighty in honour,
put out with an Argive armament of a thousand ships
from this land,
to aid their cause in battle,
uttering from their hearts a great cry for war
like vultures, who in grief
extreme for their children high above their beds
circle around,
rowed on the oarage of their wings,
having seen go for nothing the labour of guarding
the bed that held their chicks.
And on high Apollo, it may be, hears,
or Pan, or Zeus, the bird-voiced
shrill cry of these fellow dwellers in the sky
and sends on the transgressors her who brings punishment,
though late, the Erinys.
And thus are the sons of Atreus sent
against Alexander by him whose power is greater,
Zeus, guardian of host and guest; for the sake of
a woman of many men.

(Lloyd-Jones's translation)

The effect is one of startling originality, but as always in Aeschylus, what is original is the way the traditional and the new are combined. There is an interesting mixture here of Homeric and 'modern' ideas: the notion of the legal case which the 'plaintiffs' (ἀντίδικος) make against the Trojans, and the idea of the birds as 'co-residents' (μέτοικοι) of the gods are related to contemporary institutions, the latter to the regulations governing Athenian citizenship, but the language is full of echoes of the epic,[9] and behind the elaborate picture of the birds lie two Homeric similes, which deserve close attention.

But first a word on *aigupioi* (49). 'Vultures' is a makeshift translation, which carries the repellent association of feeding on corpses; but we should note that the *aigupioi* in Homer, the obvious model for the ones in Aeschylus, are quite distinct from 'ordinary' vultures, *gupes*. These are indeed looked on with horror and appear only in contexts which dwell on the fear or threat of what will happen to the corpses of dead warriors, as at *Il.* xviii 271–2 πολλοὺς δὲ κύνες καὶ γῦπες ἔδονται/Τρώων ('dogs and vultures will feed on many of the Trojans'),[10] whereas *aigupioi* are found doing the sort of things that eagles do. There is no certainty about which particular species, if any, the *aigupioi* are to be identified with —D'Arcy Thompson was no doubt right to warn that 'vultures and eagles were ill distinguished'[11]—but one thing is quite clear, that they are not associated with carrion-eating in Homer. The qualities in fact given emphasis are the aggressiveness of the *aigupios*, its noisy ferocity and its care for its young. Heroes can be favourably compared to these birds: at *Il.* xiii 531 Meriones swoops like an *aigupios* to retrieve his spear from the wounded Deiphobus: at *Il.* xvii 460 Automedon, driving Achilles' horses, rushes into battle like an *aigupios* after geese; at *Od.* xxii 302–6 there is a more developed comparison marking the killing of the suitors by Odysseus and Telemachus:

οἱ δ' ὥς τ' αἰγυπιοὶ γαμψώνυχες ἀγκυλοχεῖλαι
ἐξ ὀρέων ἐλθόντες ἐπ' ὀρνίθεσσι θόρωσι·
ταὶ μέν τ' ἐν πεδίῳ νέφεα πτώσσουσαι ἵενται,
οἱ δέ τε τὰς ὀλέκουσιν ἐπάλμενοι, οὐδέ τις ἀλκὴ
γίγνεται οὐδὲ φυγή· χαίρουσι δέ τ' ἀνέρες ἄγρῃ.

302–6

'... as *aigupioi* with hooked talons and curved beaks come from the mountains and swoop on (smaller) birds; the birds shrink from the clouds[12] and rush along the plain; the *aigupioi* leap on them and destroy them, and they have no help and no escape. Men delight in (watching) the chase'. Grim as the picture is, there is no doubt that the leading idea here is the decisive superiority of Odysseus and his followers.[13] The two similes describing the noise made by the birds are discussed below; their only other appearance in Homer is at *Il.* vii 58–61, when Athena and Apollo sit in the guise of *aigupioi* in an oak tree enjoying the sight of the battle array. Evidently the image was dignified enough for gods to assume,[14] and we should hesitate before we identify either the Homeric or the Aeschylean *aigupioi* as 'ignoble' or disgusting animals.[15] Like lions or boars, they can be used by Homer both to enhance and to demean a hero, to set him apart in his superior strength and power and to reduce him to something less than a man.[16]

Aeschylus' birds have three main functions: they make a great deal of angry noise, they have been robbed of their nestlings and suffer distress, and they are avenged by a neighbouring god, who sends a fury to punish the nest-robbers. It will be simplest to take these three aspects one by one. The sons of Atreus crying 'war' like noisy *aigupioi* recall *Il.* xvi 428-30, which describes Sarpedon and Patroclus in combat:

> οἱ δ' ὥς τ' αἰγυπιοὶ γαμψώνυχες ἀγκυλοχεῖλαι
> πέτρῃ ἐφ' ὑψηλῇ μεγάλα κλάζοντε μάχωνται,
> ὣς οἱ κεκλήγοντες ἐπ' ἀλλήλοισιν ὄρουσαν.
>
> 428-30

'. . . as *aigupioi* with hooked talons and curved beaks fight on a high rock, with loud cries, so they cried out as they rushed at one another'. The associations suggested by the Homeric echo are complex: the analogy with the fighting birds brings out the wild ferocity of Agamemnon and Menelaus and so perhaps suggests the threat of the bestial impinging on civilized life, but it also gives them heroic status. The image is applied by Homer to two of his greatest warriors, Patroclus and Sarpedon, who in the immediately following passage is singled out by his father Zeus as 'dearest of men to me'. Moreover, κλάζειν, though often used of birds and animals, is also properly applied to human beings: what Silk calls 'neutral' terminology.[17] To translate it 'scream' would perhaps tip the balance too decisively in the 'bestial' direction. Within this Parodos the word is also used of the victory cry shouted in Zeus's honour (Ζῆνα δέ τις . . . ἐπινίκια κλάζων 174) and of Calchas' prophetic utterance (ἀπέκλαγξεν 156).

The bereft creatures whose nest has been robbed tell a rather different story. Nature, 'the wild', is not any kind of threat here, but a *model* for human order, the birds representing the nurture of young by their parents. The immediate exemplar is that moving scene in the *Odyssey* where Telemachus and Odysseus recognize one another and weep as they embrace:

> κλαῖον δὲ λιγέως, ἀδινώτερον ἤ τ' οἰωνοί,
> φῆναι ἢ αἰγυπιοὶ γαμψώνυχες, οἷσί τε τέκνα
> ἀγρόται ἐξείλοντο πάρος πετεηνὰ γενέσθαι.
>
> xvi 216-18

'They cried loudly, as vehement in their grief
as birds, 'sea-eagles'[18] or *aigupioi* with
hooked talons, whose children the huntsmen
took away before they were fledged.'

We might also think of Achilles in *Il.* ix. 323–4 comparing himself and
his efforts on behalf of the Achaeans with a mother bird toiling to
bring food to her nestlings.[19] If this is inversion it is hardly inversion
of a kind that suggests the 'beast world pushing up from below'.

The third detail in the Aeschylean picture of the vultures is the
strangest and most mysterious. There is no Homeric precedent for a
god sending a fury to avenge the robbing of the vultures' nest. This is
certainly not the kind of feature one expects to find in the context of a
Homeric simile, where the description of birds and animals is
carefully naturalistic. Martin West has suggested that there may be an
echo here of the fable in Archilochus of the fox and the eagle
(fr. 177):[20] the fox persuades Zeus to punish the eagle by destroying
its offspring because the eagle has robbed the fox. However that may
be, the bold image seems also to draw on an association, traditional
and familiar in the epic, between birds and gods. The gods use bird
shapes, as in *Il.* vii 58–61, where Athena and Apollo perch on Zeus's
oak tree in the guise of *aigupioi*, and they also use birds as omens.
Sometimes god-as-bird and bird-as-omen are particularly closely
related, as when Athena/Mentor leaves Nestor and Telemachus in the
guise of a *phene* and Nestor identifies both the goddess and the
significance of her action (*Od.* iii 371–9).[21] Underlying Aeschylus'
language at 55–9 here is the assumption that the birds, because they
share in the gods' world, are special: they can function as symbols or
portents and thereby tell us something about the pattern of the world
controlled by the gods. So they provide an appropriate and indeed
authoritative context in which the idea of inevitable coming of
vengeance can be expressed, through the image of the Erinys which
dominates the trilogy.[22]

Much could be said, of course, about the relation between this
composite picture of the vultures and the other bird images in the
Oresteia: the portent of the eagles and the hare,[23] for instance, and the
language used of the prophetic Cassandra (swallow 1050, nightingale
1142–5, 'bird' 1316, swan 1444–5). But it would take us too far from
our starting point, the contribution made by the epic background to
the significance of the Aeschylean text. If I am right in arguing that
this is too complex to be neatly classified, any attempt at generaliza-
tion may be out of place, but perhaps it can be said without over-
simplification that in concentrating the different epic associations of

the *aigupioi* into a single picture Aeschylus powerfully exploits ambiguities already latent in Homer. The fierce but heroic aggression of the sons of Atreus, their painful sense of loss and outrage, the gods' mysterious power to avenge the wrongs done to them, are all evoked, but the nestlings are uncomfortably replaced by the 'woman of many husbands' (62) and we do not meet their 'true' counterparts until we are told of Iphigenia and the children of Thyestes.[24] And Aeschylus' thought-provoking use of the Homeric device of the double-ended simile (the Atridae are *both* the vultures *and* the fury sent to avenge them) is another example of his creative response to the epic material.

There is a related bird image in *Antigone* which can be discussed more briefly. The Guard's speech describing the second burial of Polynices includes a gripping account of the dust storm followed by the sudden appearance of Antigone:

καὶ τοῦδ' ἀπαλλαγέντος ἐν χρόνῳ μακρῷ,
ἡ παῖς ὁρᾶται, κἀνακωκύει πικρᾶς[25]
ὄρνιθος ὀξὺν φθόγγον, ὡς ὅταν κενῆς
εὐνῆς νεοσσῶν ὀρφανὸν βλέψῃ λέχος.

422-5

'And when, after a long while, this storm had passed, the
maid was seen; and she cried aloud with the sharp cry
of a bird in its bitterness,—even as when, within the
empty nest, it sees the bed stripped of its nestlings.'

(Jebb's translation)

What are we to make of this image of Antigone as mother bird crying over her empty nest? Segal rightly emphasizes the way it brings out Antigone's ambiguous status in relation to nature: she is unmarried, and much is made of the fact that she is being deprived of her intended marriage to Haemon, and at the same time she is the *mother* bird who has lost her nestlings and (823-32) a Niobe who forever grieves for her children.[26] Not so easy to accept is his suggestion that the use of the bird simile here reduces her to less than human status. 'In the failure of Creon's polis to mediate between beast and god the one who performs this most basic act of civilization is cast outside the pale of humanity and enters the beast world. And yet the deed done in this beastlike way may be the work of the gods'.[27] Segal bases this reading on a consideration of the bird simile along with two other details, the fact that Antigone brings the dust for the second burial of Polynices 'in her bare hands' and that she is 'hunted' by the guards.

On the first point we should note that the Greek merely has χερσίν 'with her hands' (καὶ χερσὶν εὐθὺς διψίαν φέρει κόνιν 429), which surely gives emphasis not to the animal-like nature of what she does but to the ritual act of sprinkling earth on the corpse, which has to be done with the hand.[28] We might note that when she has sprinkled the earth Antigone 'crowns' the corpse with libations from a 'well-hammered bronze urn' (ἔκ τ'εὐκροτήτου χαλκέας ἄρδην πρόχου/χοαῖσι τρισπόνδοισι τὸν νέκυν στέφει 430–1) a detail which emphasizes both the ritual propriety and the 'epic' dignity of the setting. As for Antigone as the prey of the guards (σὺν δέ νιν θηρώμεθ' 432–3), the implicit comparison with an animal victim may tell us more about what we are to imagine as the Guard's values than about Antigone's 'beastlike' way of doing the deed.

George Steiner on the same passage suggests that there is a link between Sophocles' image and the Aeschylean bereft vultures; he describes the simile as 'presumably traditional', though without pointing to any epic models. He has helpful comments to make on the interaction in the language between 'nest' and 'bed' (εὐνῆς and λέχος, 425) and on the maternal and nuptial associations this evokes. He goes on: 'The pathos of Antigone's bird-cry needs no emphasis. But the Guard's account points to areas of experience outside those which are strictly human. And this is the point. Bird-headed anthropomorphic figures, 'women as birds', be they nightingale or harpy, have their functions—consoling, devouring or ambivalent—throughout Greek myth and ritual. At its origins even the Sphinx may very likely have been a bird-woman. Antigone's shrill lament voices instincts and values older and less rational than man and man's discourse. Can the πόλις, built as it is on essential delimitations between the human and the animal spheres, fundamentally committed as it is to articulate speech, contain, give adequate echo to, such cries?'[29] Neither of these critics brings out what to me seems a crucial association, the link with Homeric poetry. In the background here, surely, are *both* the crying of Odysseus and Telemachus like vultures robbed of their young *and* the image of Achilles as mother bird, the solitary figure of *Il.* ix 323–4:

> ὡς δ' ὄρνις ἀπτῆσι νεοσσοῖσι προφέρῃσι
> μάστακ', ἐπεί κε λάβῃσι, κακῶς δ' ἄρα οἱ πέλει αὐτῇ.

'As a bird brings food to her wingless nestlings, whenever she can find any, and things go hard for her.'

We should not forget, either, the other image of Achilles as suffering parent: the lion of *Il.* xviii 318–22, roaring as it searches for the robber of its cubs. Of course Antigone's cries are linked in complex ways with the pervasive bird imagery of the rest of the play, but they are not bird cries pure and simple: Antigone is a bird as Telemachus and Odysseus and Achilles are birds, and the echoes must affect our reading. The language of the Sophoclean simile recalls not only the sorrow of bereft kin but also the isolation, suffering and intransigence of the Homeric Achilles, which I suggest are more *à propos* for our understanding of Antigone than Steiner's bird-headed women.

Much more extensive work needs to be done in order to test the claims I have been making; at least there is no shortage of relevant material.

P. E. Easterling
Newnham College, Cambridge

FOOTNOTES

[1] In (edd.) J-P. Vernant and P. Vidal-Naquet, *Mythe et tragédie en Grèce ancienne* (Paris 1973), English trans. by J. Lloyd, *Tragedy and myth in ancient Greece* (Brighton 1981) 1–5.

[2] *Cf.* J. M. Redfield, *Nature and culture in the Iliad* (Chicago 1975) 91: 'The poet's inquiry into culture is both a criticism of culture— for it shows culture to be a source of error—and an affirmation of culture—for it shows error properly punished'.

[3] 'The *Ajax* of Sophocles', *HSCP* lxv (1961) 20.

[4] *Tragedy and civilization* (Cambridge Mass. 1981) 142 and 439 n. 122.

[5] 'Supplication and hero cult in Sophocles' *Ajax*', *GRBS* xiii (1972) 154.

[6] For a Sophoclean example see my article 'The tragic Homer' *BICS* xxxi (1984) 1–8.

[7] Segal (n. 4) 3.

[8] Redfield (n. 2) 87, offers what may be a more helpful formulation: 'Through culture man has transformed his world and made it habitable, but this transformation is only partial. Primal disorder continually reasserts itself around man and within him. Disorder limits the scope of culture and leads it into internal contradiction'.

[9] In addition to the Homeric proper names there are many compound adjectives formed on the epic model (χιλιοναύτην, δεμνιοτήρη, ὑστερόποινον) and a close echo of the Homeric στρεφεδινηθέν in στροφοδινοῦνται ('a sublime transference', Fraenkel). But the differences of dialect and metre, along with non-epic words like ὀρτάλιχος and new applications of words known to Homer (e.g. ἀρωγή now in a legal as well as a military sense; see Fraenkel), create an overall effect which is very different from that of pastiche. There is no direct quotation; at 48 Page was wrong to emend μέγαν to μεγάλ' for the sake of closer correspondence with *Il.* xvi 429.

[10] *Cf. Il.* iv 237; xi 162; xvi 836, xxii 42. For the extreme horror associated with this idea cf. C. P. Segal, *The theme of the mutilation of the corpse in the Iliad* (*Mnemosyne* Suppl. 17, 1971).

[11] *A glossary of Greek birds*² (Oxford 1936) 25. For a possible (rough) identification with the bearded vulture or Lämmergeier (gypaetus barbatus) see J. Maclair Borasten, 'The birds of Homer', *JHS* xxxi (1911) 229–34; J. Pollard, *Birds in Greek life and myth* (London 1977) 79–80.

[12] The text of 304 is problematic. νέφεα looks as though it ought to be the object of πτώσσουσαι, but 'cowering from the clouds' is extremely odd. Ameis-Hentze take νέφεα as the sky, the *Wolkenbereich* where the birds have seen the predators circling round; they compare *Od*. xx 104 ὑψόθεν ἐκ νεφέων for this meaning. This is certainly better than taking νέφεα as object of ἵενται: one would expect a genitive, and in any case 'head for the clouds' is hard to reconcile with πτώσσουσαι.

[13] This was how Sophocles understood it: at *Ajax* 167–71 the Chorus compare Ajax to the great *aigupios* whose sudden appearance makes the small birds cower.

[14] *Cf*. Borasten (n. 11) 231. *Cf*. n. 18 below on the φήνη. there may be a sinister glance here at the fact that vultures watch over battlefields; but the analogy between Apollo and Athena and the predatory birds is not pressed closely. *Cf*. Redfield (n. 2) 198 on the 'buried theme' of cannibalism in the *Iliad*.

[15] As P. Vidal-Naquet does in 'Hunting and sacrifice in the *Oresteia*', Vernant and Vidal-Naquet (n. 1) 156; *cf*. M. Detienne, *The gardens of Adonis*, trans. J. Lloyd (Hassocks 1977) 23–5. The notion that an opposition between 'the noble, royal creature, the eagle of the heights' and 'the ignoble creature, the carrion eater' is relevant to the birds of the Parodos of *Agamemnon* depends on treating *aigupioi* as if they were indistinguishable from *gupes*. (It also overlooks the detail that the *aigupioi* wheel high over their nests.)

[16] For animal similes in Homer *cf*. Redfield (n. 2) 189–203; S. H. Lonsdale, *Animal imagery in Homer* (diss. Cambridge 1977); A. Schnapp-Gourbeillon, *Lions héros masques: les représentations de l'animal chez Homère* (Paris 1981).

[17] M. S. Silk, *Interaction in poetic imagery* (Cambridge 1974) 16–18, with n. 2.

[18] This is the conventional translation of φήνη, but Thompson, Borasten and Pollard (n. 11) all identify this bird more or less specifically with the bearded vulture (gypaetus barbatus). Athena turns into a φήνη at *Od*. iii 371–2.

[19] *Cf*. *Il*. xii 167–70 and xvi 259–65: wasps or bees protecting their young; xvii 4–5: Menelaus standing over the dead Patroclus like a cow over her new-born calf; xvii 132–7 Ajax shielding Patroclus like a lion protecting its young; xviii 318–22 Achilles groaning in his grief like an angry lion, as it searches for the huntsman who took away its cubs. See Redfield (n. 2) 191.

[20] '*The Parodos of the Agamemnon*', *CQ* n. s. xxix (1979) 1–2.

[21] For more examples see A. J. Podlecki, 'Omens in the *Odyssey*', *G&R* xiv (1967) 12–15.

[22] *Cf*. Silk (n. 17) 147. Redfield (n. 2) 200 sees birds as forming 'a parallel series intermediate between gods and men'.

[23] *Cf*. W. Whallon, 'Why is Artemis angry?' *AJP* 82 (1961) 80–81; Froma I. Zeitlin, 'The motif of the corrupted sacrifice in Aeschylus' *Oresteia*' *TAPA* xcvi (1965) 481–3. The eagles' offspring robbed of their parent at *Cho*. 247, 256–8 are another interesting link with *Ag*. 49–54.

[24] *Cf*. Silk (n. 17) 146–8; A. Lebeck, *The Oresteia, a study in language and structure* (Cambridge Mass. 1971) 8–9.

[25] See Jebb for a defence of πικρᾶς. R. D. Dawe argues for πικρά in *Studies on the text of Sophocles* iii (Leiden 1978) 105.

[26] Segal (n. 4) 155.

[27] Segal (n. 4) 160–1.

[28] On the religious obligation to perform at least a token act of burial on an untended corpse see R. Parker, *Miasma* (Oxford 1983) 44 and n. 44.

[29] *Antigones* (Oxford 1984) 226–7.